Bibliographic information published by the German National Library:

The German National Library lists this publication in the National Bibliography; detailed bibliographic data are available on the Internet at http://dnb.dnb.de .

Imprint:

Copyright © 2017 GRIN Verlag
Print and binding: Books on Demand GmbH, Norderstedt Germany
ISBN: 9783668648708

This book at GRIN:

https://www.grin.com/document/412010

Muhammad Waseem

An Improved and Anonymous Three-factor Authentication Key Exchange Protocol for Wireless Sensor Networks

GRIN Verlag

GRIN - Your knowledge has value

Since its foundation in 1998, GRIN has specialized in publishing academic texts by students, college teachers and other academics as e-book and printed book. The website www.grin.com is an ideal platform for presenting term papers, final papers, scientific essays, dissertations and specialist books.

Visit us on the internet:

http://www.grin.com/

http://www.facebook.com/grincom

http://www.twitter.com/grin_com

An Improved and Anonymous Three-factor Authentication Key Exchange Protocol for Wireless Sensor Networks

Department of Computer Science & Software Engineering

International Islamic University, Islamabad

September 25, 2017

MS Thesis

By:

Muhammad Waseem

A dissertation submitted to the
Department of Computer Science & Software Engineering,
International Islamic University, Islamabad
as a partial fulfillment of the requirements
for the award of the degree of
Master of Science in Computer Science.

Dedication

I dedicate this research work and feeling of gratefulness to my parents, brothers, wife and especially my loving late mother whom love and unconditional support constantly enabled me to get through the thick and thin of life.

Muhammad Waseem

Acknowledgments

With the Name of Almighty Allah, the Most Merciful, the Most Sympathetic all praise is to **ALLAH**, the Lord of the worlds, and the Holiest Man Ever Born our Prophet Mohammad (PBUH) the messenger of Allah. First and main, I should admit my limitless gratitude to Allah, the Ever-Thankful, for His helps and bless. I am absolutely persuaded that this effort would have never turn into reality, without His control.

I would also like to convey my gratitude to my research Supervisor Dr. Shehzad Ashraf Chaudhry Assistant Professor at Department of Computer-Science Software Engineering International Islamic University, Islamabad. The door to His office was at all times open when I go in difficulty or hard a query concerning my thesis. He always permitted this thesis to be my personal work, but guide me in the right direction every time he thinking I required it.

I am very appreciative to my colleagues and friends specially Mr. Fraz Ahmed Baig who has been so kind along the manner of doing my thesis.

Lastly, I should express my extremely reflective appreciation to my parents, brothers and wife for their unconditional support and nonstop encouragement during my study, researching and writing of thesis. This achievement would never achievable without them. Thank you.

Abstract

The concepts of Internet of Things (IOT) show that everything in the global network is interconnected and accessible. In IOT environment Wireless Sensor Networks (WSNs) play a very important role because of its ubiquitous nature which use for wide range of applications like military surveillance, health care, environmental monitoring, agriculture etc. WSNs consisting of large numbers of sensor nodes which sensed the sensory information from the physical phenomena and forward the same to the cluster head or gateway node, sensor node having limited battery power and cannot be recharge after deployment. WSNs are resource constraints in terms of memory, energy, computational cost and communication speed. This thesis is focus to developed light weight user authentication and key agreement protocol to access the real time information from the IOT environment. Most recently Amin et al. find out various security limitations of the Farash et al. protocol and they extended the same protocol to improve its security weaknesses and claimed that the protocol is secure in all aspects. In this thesis we scrutinized the Amin et al. protocol which reveals that the protocol still having numerous security weaknesses such as user anonymity and user traceability attacks. In response to aforementioned security limitations we designed robust smartcard base three-factor user authentication and session key agreement scheme for WSNs environment. We analyzed the novel protocol formally and informally, formal security verification has done by using BAN-Logic which show that the scheme achieve mutual authentication and session key agreement among the participant entities. Furthermore, this protocol has also simulated in popular security tool ProVerif which simulation results show that the protocol is safe and withstand against all possible attacks including the above mentioned. The performance of this scheme is also compared with associated schemes the novel protocol can be applicable in real-life applications.

Contents

1 Introduction   **2**

   1.1   One-Factor Authentication   3

   1.2   Two-Factor Authentication   4

   1.3   Three-Factor Authentication   4

   1.4   Preliminaries   4

       1.4.1   Cryptography   4

       1.4.2   Cryptanalysis   5

       1.4.3   Cryptology   5

       1.4.4   Symmetric Encryption   6

       1.4.5   Asymmetric Encryption   6

       1.4.6   One Way Hash Function   7

       1.4.7   Biohashing   8

       1.4.8   Adversarial model   8

       1.4.9   BIT Wise XOR ($\oplus$) Operation   9

   1.5   Thesis outline   10

2 Literature Review   **11**

   2.1   **Review of Amin et al. Scheme**   13

       2.1.1   System Setup Phase   14

       2.1.2   Sensor Node Registration Phase   14

       2.1.3   User Registration Phase   14

       2.1.4   Login Phase   15

       2.1.5   Authentication and the Session Key Agreement Phase   15

       2.1.6   Post-Deployment Phase   17

       2.1.7   Identity Update Phase   17

       2.1.8   Password Change Phase   17

       2.1.9   Smartcard Revocation Phase   18

2.2   Cryptanalysis and Security limitations of Amin et al.'s Scheme   19

    2.2.1   Anonymity violation and traceability attack   19

2.3   Problem Statement   21

2.4   Chapter Summary   21

3 Proposed Solution   **22**

3.1   System Setup Phase   22

3.2   Registration Phase of the Sensor Node   23

3.3   User Registration Phase   24

3.4   Login Phase   24

3.5   Authentication and Session Key Agreement Phase   25

3.6   Post Deployment Phase   28

3.7   Identity Update Phase   28

3.8   Password Change Phase   29

3.9   Smart-card Revocation Phase   29

3.10   Chapter Summary   30

4 Security Analysis   **31**

4.1   Formal Security Analysis   31

    4.1.1   Security Analysis with BAN logic   32

    4.1.2   Rules of BAN-Logic   33

    4.1.3   BAN Logic Procedure for Protocol Analysis   34

    4.1.4   ProVerif   38

4.2   Informal Security Analysis   43

    4.2.1   User Anonymity   43

    4.2.2   User Untraceability   44

    4.2.3   Stolen smart-card attack   44

    4.2.4   Replay Attack   44

    4.2.5   Off-line password guessing attack   45

    4.2.6   User-impersonation attack   45

    4.2.7   Gateway node impersonation attack   46

    4.2.8   Sensor node impersonation attack   46

    4.2.9   Privileged-insider attack   46

    4.2.10   Session key computation attack   47

    4.2.11   Verification of the session key   47

    4.2.12   Mutual Authentication   47

    4.2.13   Man-in-Middle attack   47

   4.2.14 Protection of unauthorized login 48

   4.2.15 Provision of Post-deployment phase 48

  4.3 Chapter Summary 48

5 Performance and Security comparison   **50**

  5.1 Security features comparison 50

  5.2 Computation Cost Analysis 52

  5.3 Communication Cost Analysis 52

  5.4 Storage Cost Analysis 53

  5.5 Chapter Summary 54

6 Conclusion and Future Work   **55**

List of Figures

1.1 Symmetric Cryptography 6

1.2 Asymmetric Cryptography 7

1.3 XOR Logic Circuit 9

1.4 Architecture of Network Model for user authentication in WSNs 10

2.1 Sensor node registration phase in [1] scheme 18

2.2 User registration phase in [1] scheme 19

2.3 Login and authentication phase in [1] scheme 20

3.1 Sensor node registration phase of proposed scheme 23

3.2 User Registration Phase of Proposed Scheme 25

3.3 Login and Authentication Phase of Proposed Scheme 27

List of Tables

2.1 Notation Guide 13

4.1 Notations and Concepts in BAN-Logic 32

5.1 Security requirements table 51

5.2 Comparison of computation cost and running time 53

5.3 Communication Cost of Proposed and other Protocols 53

5.4 Storage Cost Analysis 54

Chapter 1

Introduction

In the recent past, Wireless Sensor Networks (WSNs) are ever-present and using in a wide range of applications domains, like healthcare, disaster management, environmental mentoring, domestic, surveillance [2] security and agriculture. WSNs are containing small nodes which having the capabilities to sense, communicate and compute. Though early sensor-nodes were resource limited with restricted capabilities, but with the advancement of sensor hardware technology and time made it possible to prolonged their battery life memory and processing power [3]. Practically, the majority reservations in WSN applications are concerned at the gateway or from the back-end of the appliance scheme. Though, in different purposes, real time information may not access from the gateway-node just, but also be admittance in ad-hoc manner from any sensor login node. User authentication is critical whereas accessing the real time information. Thus, we need a strong authentication schemes in order to resist unauthorized user from accessing real-time data. However, so far few schemes have been proposed which are well suitable for WSNs [4].

In the start it was thinking that the WSN consisting only homogenous network means identical sensor nodes in terms of power capability etc are used but latterly found heterogeneous Wireless Sensor Networks which makes from dissimilar sort of nodes with different capability, in which some of nodes are more powerful computationally than other nodes e.g. gateway nodes. In terms of IOT notation, the variety of WSNs is not simply adopting, that's why the communications is stimulated from main infrastructure based network in which node only communicate to the gateway node, to ad-hoc networks whereas node are also corresponded directly with another node[5].

WSNs are still becoming more frequent and organized by way of IOT, thus demonstrated novel opportunity but also challenge which is required to be tackling. An instance of such would be an isolated user who desires to admittance a specific sensor-node of the WSNs. So this type of user requires to be allowed and, if made completely, permitted to collect data from or send instructions to the sensor-node. Ever since the majority significant and different quality of WSNs is their resource-limited structural design (i.e., restricted communicational and computational power), a lightweight security clarification is necessary, so urging the protection plan to be more practical [6]. An example of such, if remote users want to access a particular node or real time data from the concerned node, such a user requires fist to authorized that positively allowed to access or collect information from the concerned end. While the most essential issues of the WSNs are resource constraint architecture (i.e. restricted communicational and computational capability), hence a lightweight defense solution is obligatory, therefore the influence of the security proposes to be extra sensible.

In two-factor authentication protocol [1] user favor low entropy because of their tow-factor, password and smart-card. But in tow-factor authentication adversary execute the off-line password guessing threat in polynomial moment. Hence, two-factor authentications cannot afford enough safety because of offline password guessing assault. In addition three-factor authentications protocols were developed which hold up on password, smart-card and biometric (e.g. fingerprint, retina iris) have achieved reputations. So security within this authentication is very strong because biometric information cannot be guessed easily, biometric information also not forgotten easily. Huang et al. [7] proposed three-factor authentication frame work for the protection of password guessing attack of two factor authentication and upgraded the same to three-factor authentication and tackle the guessing of password attack. Three-factor authentication using biohashing operation, generating protect template of biometric.

1.1 One-Factor Authentication

One-factor authentication developed in 1981 by Lamport for the security of information, in one factor authentication used only secure password/PIN code. It is also called single factor authentication SFA user credentials/Id and password was not more secure. Other difficulty PIN code-based authentications are need understand the carefulness to generate and keep in mind strong passwords. It is also required security from internal and external threat. PIN code/Passwords have the main familiar form of one factor authentication with small cost.

1.2   Two-Factor Authentication

Two-factor authentication actually used two authentication factors in two steps verification system, this authentication is provides extra layer of protection and formulates its complex for adversary to enter a person's, online accounts and devices because password alone was not sufficient for strong security. Therefore, Two-factor authentication have been exercised to protect access to susceptible information and online organizations, ever more introducing this authentication to protect their user data from whose password has been stolen or hacked from database or otherwise.

1.3   Three-Factor Authentication

Two-factor authentication practice [1] which depends on PIN code and smart-card, users usually used low-entropy password which is uncomplicated so as a result the adversary carry out off-line password guessing risk which guess the password of user's in polynomial time. Thus, two-factor authentication scheme cannot give high level protections due to the risk of off-line password guess-sing attack. Therefore, three-factor authentication schemes were developed which is based on PIN code, smart-card and biometrics (finger-print, retina and iris) have so gained esteem. In these three-factor authentication scheme, user gets pleasure from superior safety than a two-factor method as (i) biometric information is not guessed easily (ii) biometric information is not forgotten.

1.4   Preliminaries

In this section the basic three-factor authentication architecture and background for symmetric encryption have been described:-

1.4.1   Cryptography

Cryptography is actually the conversion of legible and understandable information into a shape which is unable to understand in order to protect the data. Cryptography refers precisely the techniques for hiding the message contents, the word of cryptography has been derived from a Grecian word Kryptos which means secret and graphikos that means writing. So the following are some main terminology of cryptography[8].

Plain Text: The data that we require to hide from view is known as plaintext (P), it is the original data or text, it might be in a shape of characters, mathematical data, executable program, image, or any extra kind of data. The plain text for instance is the initial draft of messages in the dispatcher before encryption, otherwise it is a text by the side of the receiver after the decryption.

Cipher text: The information that will be sending out is described as cipher text (C), it is a word which refers to the "meaningless" string information, or indistinct text that nobody have to understand, excluding the receiver. It is the information that will be sent out accurately through network, several algorithms are used to change plain text into cipher text[9]. Cipher is actually the algorithms which use to change the plain text into cipher text, this technique is known as encryption or (encode), in other terms, it is a technique for exchanging readable and explicable information into "meaningless" information, and moreover it is represented as under:

$$C = E_{(}K)(P)$$

Where C is a cipher text, $E_{(}K)$ is an encoding algorithm by using K key and P is a plain text. The reverse of cipher process is known as decipher (decode). It is the mechanism which recovers the coded text, this scheme is known as decryption, in additional terms it is the system of exchanging "meaningless" information into legible information.

$$P = D(K^{-1})(C)$$

1.4.2   Cryptanalysis

Cryptanalysis deals with the study of encryption and already encrypted information for the objective to find out the hidden messages. Cryptanalyst can attempt any or these entire assaults (i) attempt for breaking of single message (ii) attempt to identify arrangements in encoded messages, to find out the successive ones by using straightforward decryption algorithm (iii) attempt to catch general flaws in an encryption algorithm, lacking of unavoidably having captured any message.

1.4.3   Cryptology

Cryptology is the study of both cryptanalysis and cryptography.

1.4.4   Symmetric Encryption

Symmetric Encryption is that type of cryptosystem in which the similar key used for encoding and decoding. Key plays significant role in this encryption. The distribution of the key should be done before communication between entities [10]. This encryption procedure is also known as single key or conventional encryption. There are numerals advantages of this method. Performance is comparatively more than other. In this technique having two main features, encryption algorithm and key. The encryption algorithm change plain text to cipher text by using the secret key and encryption algorithm. In the process of decryption the same process of encryption are used but in reverse order with the similar key. A robust algorithm should be contingent on its key exclusively. The flaws of symmetric algorithms are in distribution of symmetric key among the sender and receiver [11].

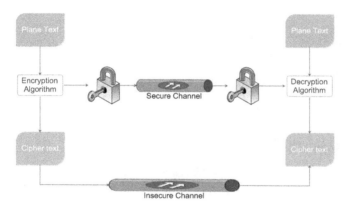

Figure 1.1: Symmetric Cryptography

1.4.5   Asymmetric Encryption

Diffie and Helman was discover innovative encryption formula in 1976 which is known as asymmetric encryption or public key encryption. Asymmetric encryption is dissimilar than symmetric encryption in security, because it does not share the secret key between the dispatcher and the recipient, this is the key difference between asymmetric and symmetric encryption. In this encryption process the sender have the public key of the recipient and the receiver has its own private key which is not possible to find via the public key, so there is no need to share the key. It is the responsibility of the receiver to established public and his private key, also the receiver transmit the public key to every senders by some channel. He wants even public channels to deliver his asymmetric key or public key can use whichever the secret key or public to encrypt/decrypt the information. Public key encryption might be used to employ the authentication and non-repudiation security performance, it can also use for digital signature and further purpose that never be execute with symmetric encryption. Asymmetric encryption is very complicated and slower in computation than symmetric encryption. So, asymmetric encryption deal plaintext like a collection of numbers which are operated in mathematics, whereas the plaintext in symmetric encryption deal as collection of characters and symbol, the encryption procedure may transpose these symbols, or may replace one symbol by another[12].

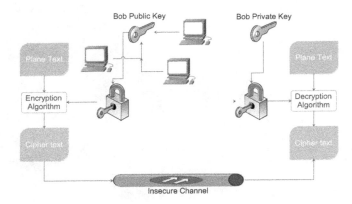

Figure 1.2: Asymmetric Cryptography

1.4.6 One Way Hash Function

In the mechanism of this function H: $\{0,1\}^* \rightarrow Y_q^*$ which takes a variable length of data 'M' as an input and produced fixed size of code/cryptogram C=H(M), the fixed size output 'C' lexis which is known as hash code. So a small change in 'M' produced considerable change in 'C' [10]. The main properties of hash function are as under:-

- It is easy computationally to get C = H (M), when M is known.

- It is infeasible computationally to calculate M, when C = H(M) is known.

- It is complicated to get two inputs M and T like H (M) = H (T). Thus this state is called collision-resistance state.

Definition 1: A hash function be a identical fellowships $F=C_n$ of tracks of range polynomial into n, taking input of range n and produce output of range $m < n$. So this function family unit be a hash function because the input is separated into two parts, x plus k, so as to n is polynomial in$| x |$ and $m <| x |$ [13].

1.4.7 Biohashing

The conception of Bio-Hashing is actually system of cancellable/disposable biometrics procedure. In this method, a Biometric features are integrated with user specific random numbers to deals the performance and security of the biometric system. In BioHashing method, the fingerprint data of user are result to store in extremely interrelated bit strings. Additionally in this technique the user particular code cannot be obtained by the adversary[14]. Thus this bio-hashing feature would secure our scheme beside any biometric improbable. Thus the illegal users can simply recognized by this mechanism. This tactic delivers the revocable characteristics in the biometric. Thus the chances of disclose of the real biometric pattern are abolished. Therefore, BioHashing has important beneficial advantages more than exclusively biometrics mistake rate point as well as clear division of the authentic and fraudulent people. The anticipated Biohashing methodology utilized non-invertibility procedure for enhanced safety along with performance [15].

1.4.8 Adversarial model

In this thesis common adversarial model contain all possible assumptions of the adversary as mentioned in [16]. According to the potential of the adversary $\mathcal{A}$ all possible assumption made by the adversary described as following:-

1. $\mathcal{A}$ have complete control over the public channel, so $\mathcal{A}$ is capable to interrupt, modify, reply, takeout or can also send a fresh fabricated message.

2. $\mathcal{A}$ can also extract the smartcard information by power analysis or leak the same.

3. $\mathcal{A}$ can be external stranger or malicious insider user of the same system.

4. The insider known the ID of the register users and server because these are public.

5. Servers are usually understood to be safe but $\mathcal{A}$ cannot negotiate any server of the entire system (i.e. Secret key is not accessible to adversary).

1.4.9 BIT Wise XOR ($\oplus$) Operation

A simple XOR cipher is use in cryptography which is a form of preservative cipher, an encoding technique that functions according to the given standard.

$0 \oplus 0 = 0,\ 0 \oplus 1 = 1,\ 1 \oplus 0 = 1,\ 1 \oplus 1 = 0$

From the above principles show that result is *true* either one of the input is *true*, but not both. The result is *false* when both the inputs are *true* or if both the inputs are *false*. Simply it examine that the result is 1 if the inputs are dissimilar, otherwise 0 if the input are the similar.

It is a main plus point of XOR that easy to employ, besides the XOR process is inexpensive computationally. In simple XOR operation in which the same key is use for XOR process on the total data this cipher is use for secure information in those cases wherever specific security is is needed. When keys are random and are at smallest along with the message, then XOR encoding is greatly secure than as the key replication in a message. While the key stream is produced through the random-number generator, then outcome be stream cipher by using really random key with the key that is really random, the outcome is one tim-pade which are strong even in idea.

Symbol	Truth Table		
	B	A	Q
	0	0	0
A ○———⟩⟩=1○ Q B ○———⟩⟩ 2-input Ex-OR Gate	0	1	1
	1	0	1
	1	1	0
Boolean Expression Q = A B	A OR B but NOT BOTH gives Q		

Figure 1.3: XOR Logic Circuit

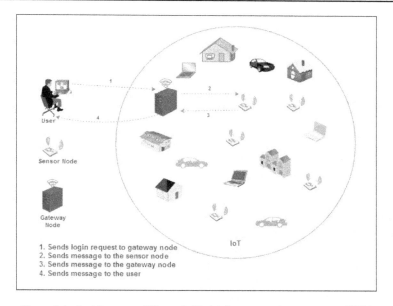

Figure 1.4: Architecture of Network Model for user authentication in WSNs

1.5 Thesis outline

Further arrangement of thesis are as under:-

- Chapter 2, We discussed the literature study of previous papers, review of [1],detailed examination as well cryptanalysis of Amin et al.'s. In the last of chapter 2 we have been presented the problem statement of our research.

- Chapter 3, We presented the proposed solution which consisting of total nine phases.

- Chapter 4, We discussed the safety analysis of our scheme, we asses the same protocol formally with BAN logic and ProVerif as well informally analysis beside all possible attacks.

- Chapter 5, We write down the performance analysis of the improved protocol.

- Finally, we provided conclusion and future work in Chapter 6.

Chapter 2

Literature Review

Watro et al.[17] formed a user authentication protocol in 2004, with the name of Tiny-PK using Diffie-Hellman and RSA algorithm but the Tiny-PK scheme vulnerable to masquerade attack (the session key was encrypted by intruders alongwith new parameters and transmit encrypted data to the end user) but this protocol cannot capable to opposes man-in-the middle attack. Wong et al.[18] lunched forceful user authentication protocol in 2006 for WSNs using the hash function, this scheme permitted legitimate user to each sensor node at the network but Wong et al.[18] protocol is vulnerable to forgery and replay attack. Later on in 2007 Tseng et al.[6] improve Wong et al.[18] scheme and proposed improve user authentication scheme and enhanced the security flaws of Wong et al.'s scheme Tseng et al.'s[6] having four man phases, Registration , Login, Authentication and Password Change Phase but the Tseng et al.'s having some security flaws with different malicious attack.

He et al.[19], in 2010 stated the weaknesses of M.L.Das's[20], protocol which was suffered from impersonation attack, insider attack and their password cannot change by the user. He et al. then enhanced the existing scheme with two factor authentication and reveal the weaknesses of Das's protocol. He et al. scheme is vulnerable to leakage of information attack, non-preservation of user-anonymity, the session key cannot be recognized between the sensor node and user also this scheme has lack of mutual authentication stuck between the sensor-node and the user. Fan et al.[9] suggested a schemes which was uncomplicated user authentication protocol, which withstand denial of services (DoS) also resist user authentication protocol, this scheme established the session key stuck between the user and cluster node (header node) in WSNs. Vaidya et al.[21], stated that M.L.Das's[20] protocol and Khan-Alghatbar's[22] schemes having some security fault and vulnerable to different attacks, consisting of stolen smart-card attack, to overcome these security flaws of both protocols proposed tow-factor authentication schemes which is portent smart card theft attack and other familiar kinds of vulnerabilities.

In current era bio-metric user authentication also focus some research concentration. Yuan et al.[23], suggested a biometric authentication of user for WSN using the idea of M.L.Das's schemes. In this scheme GWN node cannot accept any acknowledgment in their scheme, furthermore, the sensor node and getaway node cannot known the message if attacker block it from accomplishment the node. The same scheme is also not flexible against node negotiation attack, but support freely changing of password on local based containing with the gateway node in the network as matched with other scheme. Xu et al.[24] and Song proposed a user authentication protocol which based on RSA and Diffie-Hellman to get the mutual authentication property. But the drawback of [24] schemes are overhead of memory because these protocols store all the public key of a node as well the user. To overcome the drawbacks of these protocols in 2011 Yeh et al.[25] proposed another ECC based asymmetric cryptographic protocol for WSNs. Kumar-Lee[26], pointed out some flaws of He et al.[19] scheme does not proved session key institution and mutual authentication connecting sensor node plus user. Kumar-Lee also stated that the He et al.[19] protocol have lack of user anonymity and information leakage attack. They also found absence of session key and mutual authentication in Khan-Algathber's scheme [22]. Ashok Kumar Das et al.[27], in 2012 proposed a hierarchical WSN user authentication protocol based on dynamic password, in this scheme the real time data can be right of entry from the nodes, because the real-time information are not only access through bas-station, so access are given to the outside user (parties) only to those who allowed to get information when they required. Hence authentication performs a very important role for the same purposes. This scheme also change password dynamically without base-station getaway node help as well support dynamic node addition.

Turkanovic and Holbl[28], assert Das et al.[27] protocol is imperfect proposing enhanced protocols Turkanovic and Holbl and Li et al[29] but these protocols also not withstand all possible vulnerabilities. Recently, in 2014 Turkanovic et al.[5], proposed a lightweight user authentication protocol which based on hash-function and using the concept of IOT, with heterogeneous ad-hoc WSN. The main objective of this protocol was anonymity and energy efficiency with low computation cost and high security. However, Farash et al.[30], and Ruul and Biswas[2] stated that this protocols are not suitable for the realistic application due to it security weaknesses. Moreover, Rulul and Biswas using smart-card proposed user authentication protocol which was multi getaway based. In recent time Farash et al.[30] developed an improve protocol which also examined that this protocol cannot withstand offline password guessing threat, stolen smart-card attack, user anonymity problem, session

Table 2.1: Notation Guide

Notations	Description
U_i	User
SN	Sensor Node
SA	System Administrator
SCN	Unique Smartcard number
GN	Gateway Node
PW_{ui}	Password of User
ID_{ui}	Identity of User
ID_{SN}	Identity of SN
X_{GN-SN}	Shared Key between GN and SN
X_{GN}	Secret Key of GN
X_{SN}	Secret Key of SN
r_i	Random No generated by U_i
r_s	Random No generated by SN
T_x	Timestamp of user x
fng_i	Biometric template of U_i
$\triangle T$	Constant Transmission delay
SK	Session Key of the Protocol
$E_{X_{GN}}$	Symmetric Encryption with X_{GN}
$D_{X_{GN}}$	Symmetric Decryption with X_{GN}
B_{ui}	Biometric Key of fng_i, where B_{ui}=BK(H(fng_i))
$\oplus$	The XOR operation
$h(.)$	one-way hash function
$\|$	The concatenation operation

explicit transitory information attack and password guessing attack. Recently Amin et al.'s[1] suggested a three-factor IoT based authentication scheme for the achievement of security loophole in Farash et al.[30] in which they also claimed the anonymity. But after the insight perusal we scrutinized that the Amin et al.'s[1] protocol is still having user anonymity and user traceability attack detail review and cryptanalysis of [1] are as under:-

2.1 Review of Amin et al. Scheme

This scheme[1] consisting of total nine phases: System Setup Phase, Sensor Node Registration, User Registration, Login, Authentication and Session Key Agreement, Post Deployment, Identity Update, Password Change and Smartcard Revocation Phase these all are narrated as under.

2.1.1 System Setup Phase

The System Administrator SA performed this mode off-line, which comprising the following steps:

Step 1: SA selects the identity ID_{SN} of $SN(1 \leq j \leq m)$

Step 2: A master key X_{GN} chosen by SA this key only known GN and computes $X_{SN} = h(ID_{SN}||X_{GN})$, X_{SN} is the secret key of SN which is unique for each SN.

Step 3: A random number R_{shrd}, is selected by SA and shared between SN and GN. SA finally stored $\{ID_{SN}, X_{SN}, R_{shrd}\}$ in temper proof memory of SN.

2.1.2 Sensor Node Registration Phase

After the setup phase the SA deploy the sensor node SN and single GN on the target area to make sensor network this phase as shown in figure 2.1 steps of the same phase are describe below:

Step 1: A SN computes S_1 and S_2, $S_1 = ID_{SN} \oplus h(R_{shrd}||T_1)$, $S_2 = h(ID_{SN}||X_{SN}||R_{shrd}||T_1)$ then send S_1 and S_2 with timestamp T_{s1} via an unreliable channel with fresh time stamp to GN.

Step 2: GN verify these parameters with timestamp $\mid T_{GN} - T_{s1} \mid \leq \Delta T$ hold. If incorrect the GN rejects SN, otherwise computing $ID'_{SN} = S_1 \oplus h(R_{shrd} \parallel T_{s1})$, $X'_{SN} = h(ID'_{SN}||X_{GN})$, and $S'_2 = h(ID'_{SN} \parallel X'_{SN} \parallel R_{shrd} \parallel T_{s1})$ to check whether $S'_2 = S_2$ holds. If false the GN rejects the SN otherwise SN are authenticates by GN and stored ID_{SN} in memory.

Step 3: The confirmation message send to SN by GN after successful completion of registration phase and R_{shrd} are deleted by SN from memory.

2.1.3 User Registration Phase

This phase is illustrated in figure 2.2.

Step 1: A user U_i chosen an identity ID_{ui} send it alongwith personal credential via an unreliable channel to SA, personal credential support in re-issuing of fresh smart-card for U_i whose smart-card are either damage or stolen.

Step 2: SA check the previous ID_{ui} in record if exist, it request for fresh identity; otherwise computes $d_i = h(ID_{ui} \parallel X_{GN})$ and $L_i = h(SCN \parallel X_{GN})$, then store $\{d_i, L_i, SCN,$ BK()$\}$ in smart-card and send it to user through reliable channel. Here BK() is the biometric extraction and key generation function, SA keep a table in which store ID_{ui} and personal information of each user.

Step 3: U_i entered the smart-card in the card reader. U_i enters (ID_{ui}, PW_{ui}) and fingerprint fng_{ui} through sensor device to smart-card. Then the smart-card compute $B_{ui} = BK(H(fng_{ui})), e_{ui} = h(ID_{ui}\|PW_{ui} \parallel B_{ui}), f_{ui} = d_i \oplus h(ID_{ui}\|PW_{ui})$ and $g_{ui} = L_i \oplus h(PW_{ui} \oplus ID_{ui})$, here H(.) is a bio-hashing process. Smart-card store $\{$ $B_{ui}, e_{ui}, f_{ui}, g_{ui}, SCN, BK()\}$ in its memory and deleted (d_i, l_i).

2.1.4 Login Phase

When a register user want to get the real-time information it need to login with GN to access information. Narrative of this phase are given in figure 2.3:-

Step 1: U_i enter the smart-card in the card-reader and captured its fingerprint fng_{ui} through sensor device, then smart-card computes: $B_{ui}^* = BK(H(fng_{ui}))$, also check where $B_{ui}^* = B_{ui}$. If it is not equal then Smart-card deny the login request of U_i, otherwise it request for identity and password of U_i. The U_i enter ID_{ui} and PW_{ui} to smart-card and computes $e_{ui}^* = h(ID_{ui} \parallel PW_{ui} \parallel B_{ui})$ smart-card reject the login request of U_i if $e_{ui}^* \neq e_{ui}$ otherwise, $ID_{ui}^* = ID_{ui}$ and $PW_{ui}^* = PW_{ui}$ hold.

Step 2: If U_i are valid and legitimate then the smart-card calculates $d_i^* = f_i \oplus h(ID_{ui}^* \parallel PW_{ui}^*)$ and $L_i^* = g_i \oplus h(PW_{ui}^* \oplus ID_{ui}^*)$. Smart-card also generate timestamp T_1 and random number r_i to computes: $M_1 = ID_{ui}^* \oplus h(L_i^*\|T_1)$, $M_2 = r_i \oplus h(d_i^*\|T_1)$, $M_3 = h(d_i^* \parallel r_i \parallel T_1)$ and $SCT_i = SCN \oplus h(T_1)$. The smart-card ask the identity of sensor node from U_i, sensor node SN chosen by U_i and send ID_{SN} to smart-card.

Step 3: Smart-card computes $EID_{SN} = ID_{SN} \oplus h(ID_{ui}\|r_i\|T_1)$ and send to GN $MSG_1 = (M_1, M_2, M_3, T_1, SCT_x, EID_{SN})$ using an un-reliable channel.

2.1.5 Authentication and the Session Key Agreement Phase

This phase presented the authentication process as well as session key agreement are executing among U_i, GN and SN. The narrative of this phase is illustrated in figure 2.3.

Step 1: A login message MSG_1 received to GN from U_i then GN computes $SCN = SCT_i \oplus h(T_1), L_i^/ = h(SCN \parallel X_{GN}), ID_{ui}^/ = M_1 \oplus h(L_i^/ \parallel T_1), d_i^/ = h(ID_{ui}^/ \parallel X_{GN}), r_i^/ = M_2 \oplus h(d_i^/ \parallel T_1)$ and $M_3^/ = h(d_i^/ \parallel r_i^/ \parallel T_1)$. The GN abort the session if $M_3^/ \neq M_3$. otherwise computes $M_4 = h(ID_{ui} \parallel d_i^/ \parallel T_1)$ and send $MSG_2 = (M_4)$ using an unreliable channel to U_i.

Step 2: U_i computes $M_4^* = h(ID_{ui} \parallel d_i^* \parallel T_1)$, and abort the session by U_i if M_4^* is not equal to M_4 otherwise compute $M_5 = h(d_i^* \parallel ID_{ui} \parallel r_i \parallel T_1)$ and send $MSG_3 = (M_5)$ via an unreliable channel to GN.

Step 3: GN received M_5 and compute $M_5^/ = h(d_i^/ \parallel ID_{ui}^/ \parallel r_i^/ \parallel T_1)$, and abort the session if $M_5^* \neq M_5$, otherwise sure that attacker does not lunch any reply attack.

Step 4: In order to check legitimacy of U_i, GN to SN, GN computes $ID_{SN}^/ = EID_{SN} \oplus h(ID_{ui} \parallel r_i \parallel T_1)$, $X_{SN}^/ = h(ID_{sn}^/ \parallel X_{GN})$, $M_6 = h(ID_{ui}^/ \parallel ID_{SN}^/ \parallel ID_{GN} \parallel X_{SN}^/ \parallel r_i^/ \parallel T_2)$, $M_7 = ID_{ui}^/ \oplus h(ID_{GN} \parallel X_{SN}^/ \parallel T_2)$ and $M_8 = r_i \oplus h(ID_{ui}^/ \parallel X_{SN}^/)$ and send $MSG_4 = \{ID_{GN}, M_6, M_7, M_8, T_2\}$ via an unreliable channel to SN.

Step 5: SN check true timestamp $\mid T_3 - T_2 \mid \leq \triangle T$ holds, when the same is false SN immediately reject the session otherwise compute: $ID_{ui}^{**} = M_7 \oplus h(ID_{GN} \parallel X_{SN} \parallel T_2)$, $r_i^{**} = M_8 \oplus h(ID_{ui}^{**} \parallel X_{SN})$ and $M_6^{**} = h(ID_{ui}^{**} \parallel ID_{SN} \parallel ID_{GN} \parallel X_{SN} \parallel r_i^{**} \parallel T_2)$, SN also terminate the connection if $M_6^{**} \neq M_6$, otherwise it trust that U_i and GN are authentic entities. Moreover, SN computes: $SK_{sn} = h(ID_{ui}^{**} \parallel ID_{SN} \parallel r_i^{**} \parallel r_s)$, $M_9 = h(SK_{sn} \parallel X_{SN} \parallel r_s \parallel T_3)$ and $M_{10} = r_i^{**} \oplus r_s$ and send $MSG_5 = \{M_9, M_{10}, T_3\}$ to GN via an unreliable channel.

Step 6: GN check the timestamps T_4 which is current timestamp or not if it is false the GN terminate the session, otherwise it computes: $r_s^/ = M_{10} \oplus r_i, SK_{GN} = h(ID_{ui}^/ \parallel ID_{SN} \parallel r_i^/ \parallel r_S^/)$ and $M_9^/ = h(SK_{GN} \parallel S_{SN}^/ \parallel r_S^/ \parallel T_3)$, GN abort the session if $M_9^/$ is not equal to M_9, otherwise compute $M_{11} = h(SK_{GN} \parallel ID_{ui}^/ \parallel d_i \parallel r_S^/)$ and send $MSG_6 = \{M_{11}, M_{10}\}$ via an unreliable channel to U_i.

Step 7: U_i computes $r_S^* = M_{10} \oplus r_i, SK_{ui} = h(ID_{ui} \parallel ID_{SN} \parallel r_i \parallel r_S^*), M_{11}^* = h(SK_{ui} \parallel ID_{ui} \parallel d_i \parallel r_s)$ so terminating the session if $M_{11}^* \neq M_{11}$ otherwise U_i trust on authenticity between GN and SN. This protocol then establish session key $SK_i = SK_{sn} = SK_{GN}$ between U_i, S_i and GN after mutual authentication.

2.1.6 Post-Deployment Phase

The purposes of subject phase is deployment of sensor nodes to forming a Network. If one or more node may be damage so this damage node S_k replaced with a new node S_{new} on the target field. SA select ID_{new} and S_{new} to complete $X_{new} = h(ID_{new}||X_{GN})$ and embed this $(ID_{new}, X_{new}, R_{shrd})$ in memory of S_{new}.

2.1.7 Identity Update Phase

The main focus of this phase is the security to updates the identity of the registered user this phase required help of GN the legitimacy of U_i verify in login phase GN and smart-card compute the following:-

Step 1: U_i insert the smart-card in the card reader and input his new ID_{ui}^{new} then smart-card computes: $d_i^* = f_{ui} \oplus h(ID_{ui}||PW_{ui})$, $L_i^* = g_{ui} \oplus h(PW_{ui} \oplus ID_{ui})$, $Z_i = h(d_i^*||ID_{ui}||T_{id})$, $W_i = ID_{ui} \oplus h(L_i||T_{id})$, $SCT_x = SCN \oplus h(T_{id})$ and $DD_{ui} = ID_{ui}^{new} \oplus h(L_i||d_i||T_{id})$. Then the smart-card store $\{Z_i, W_i, DD_{ui}, SCT_x, T_{id}\}$ and send to GN via unreliable channel.

Step 2: Then GN computes $SCN = SCT_x \oplus h(T_{id})$, $L_i^/ = h(SCN||X_{GN})$, $ID_{ui}^/ = W_i \oplus h(L_i^/||T_{id})$, $d_i^/ = d_i^/ = h(ID_{ui}^/||X_{GN})$ and $Z_i^/ = Z_i$ hold if true then GN computes: $ID_{ui}^{new} = DD_i \oplus h(L_i^/||d_i^/||T_{id})$, $d_i^{**} = h(ID_{ui}^{new}||X_{GN})$, $Y_{ui} = d_i^{**} \oplus d_i^/$ and $ZZ_i = h(d_i^{**}||Z_i^/)$ and send (ZZ_i, Y_{ui}) to smart-card via an unreliable channel, and also updates new Id in Database.

Step 3: In this step smart-compute $d_i^{**} = Y_{ui} \oplus d_i^/$, $ZZ_i^* = h(d_i^{**}||Z_i)$ and checks $ZZ_i^* = ZZ_i$ holds, if is true then smart-card compute $e_{ui}^{new} = h(ID_{ui}^{new}||PW_{ui}||B_{ui})$, $f_{ui}^{new} = d_i^{**} \oplus h(ID_{ui}^{new}||PW_{ui})$ and $g_{ui}^{new} = L_i \oplus h(PW_{ui} \oplus ID_{ui}^{new})$ then old information are replace by smart-card $\{e_{ui}, f_{ui}, g_{ui}\}$ with new information $(e_{ui}^{new}, f_{ui}^{new}, g_{ui}^{new})$ which store on the smart-card.

2.1.8 Password Change Phase

For the security enhancement the registered user U_i want to modify his/her password with-out the assistance of SA and GN. This phase express as under:-

Step 1: U_i insert his smart-card within the card-reader and process step 1 of the login phase and verify password, identity and fingerprints.

Step 2: The Smart-card indicate U_i for the input of a new password, PW_{ui}^{new}, U_i input new password PW_{ui}^{new} so the smart-card computes $e_{ui}^{new} = h(ID_{ui}||PW_{ui}^{new}||B_{ui})$, $d_i' = f_{ui} \oplus h(ID_{ui}||PW_{ui})$, $f_{ui}^{new} = d_{ui}^{new} \oplus h(ID_{ui}||PW_{ui}^{new})$, $L_i' = g_{ui} \oplus h(PW_{ui} \oplus ID_{ui})$ and $g_{ui}^{new} = L_i' \oplus h(PW_{ui}^{new} \oplus ID_{ui})$.

Step 3: Smart-card update the old information (e_{ui}, g_{ui}, f_{ui}) with new $\{e_{ui}^{new}, g_{ui}^{new}, f_{ui}^{new}\}$ in smart-card memory the rest of parameter keep unchanged.

2.1.9 Smartcard Revocation Phase

When the registered user smart-card may be stolen or lost this protocol issue the new smart-card by performing the below steps.

Step 1: U_i send his identity ID_{ui} alongwith personal detail to the concern SA via a reliable channel. SA verify U_i credentials if valid then compute: $d_i^{new} = h(ID_{ui}||X_{GN})$ and $L_i^{new} = h(SCN^{new}||X_{GN})$, SCN^{new} is a unique number of new smart-card. The SA store $\{d_i^{new}, L_i^{new}, SCN^{new}, BK()\}$ in the memory of new smart-card and send it securely to user. SA update the Database with SCN^{new}.

Step 2: The U_i insert smart-card, input ID_{ui}, password PW_{ui} and input fingerprint with device and computes: $B_{ui}^{new} = BK(H(fng_{ui}))$, $e_{ui}^{new} = h(ID_{ui}||PW_{ui}||B_{ui}^{new})$, $f_{ui}^{new} = d_{ui}^{new} \oplus h(ID_{ui}||PW_{ui})$ and $g_{ui}^{new} = L_i^{new} \oplus h(PW_{ui} \oplus ID_{ui})$. Finally Smart-card store $(B_{ui}^{new}, e_{ui}^{new}, f_{ui}^{new}, g_{ui}^{new}, SCN^{new}, BK())$ in its memory and delete $\{d_{ui}^{new} L_{ui}^{new}\}$ from memory.

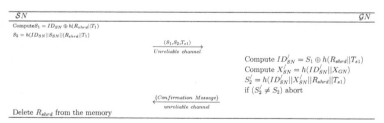

Figure 2.1: Sensor node registration phase in [1] scheme

$\mathcal{U}_i/Smartcard$	SA
Chose ID_{ui}	

$\xrightarrow{\{ID_{ui},Personal\ credential\}}$
reliable channel

If ID_{ui} is found in the database
Request another identity
Else, Compute $d_i = h(ID_{ui}||X_{GN})$
Compute $L_i = h(SCN||X_{GN})$
Store $(d_i, L_i, SCN, BK())$ into smart-card

$\xleftarrow{\{Smartcard\}}$
reliable channel

Input (ID_{ui},PW_{ui}) into smartcard
Input fng_{ui} at sensor device
Compute $B_{ui} = BK(H(fng_{ui}))$
Compute $f_{ui} = d_i \oplus h(ID_{ui}||PW_{ui})$
Compute $e_{ui} = h(ID_{ui}||PW_{ui}||B_{ui})$
Compute $g_{ui} = L_i \oplus h(PW_{ui} \oplus ID_{ui})$
Store $(B_{ui}, e_{ui}, f_{ui}, g_{ui}, SCN, BK())$
and drop (d_i, L_i) from the smartcard

Figure 2.2: User registration phase in [1] scheme

2.2 Cryptanalysis and Security limitations of Amin et al.'s Scheme

The Amin et al.'s[1] protocol based on three-factor authentication for the anonymity preservation and key exchange protocol for WSN. We examined that the R. Amin et al.'s protocol is suffering with some serious flaws.

2.2.1 Anonymity violation and traceability attack

In addition with conventional security, user privacy and anonymity has an enormously emergent and important factor to be considered. Lacking of anonymity and privacy the user private information may be access by adversary through just investigating the session information such private information can be distorted by the adversary. In the present time of persistent computing, user's private information which can be obtained by an attacker with examining the session specific information. In WSN Networks, the adversary becomes capable to get the moving history and location of participant user's. For the provision of anonymity an authentication scheme should be achieve after the accomplishment of these two major goals: (a) actual identity of user is never exposed to adversary (b) also the adversary not able to find out the different sessions whichever initiate by similar user. An authorized user U_i can able to break the anonymity by performing the following.

$\mathcal{U}_i/Smartcard$	$\mathcal{G}N$	SN
Inpute fng_i		
Compute $B_{ui}^* = BK(H(fng_{ui}))$		
if $(B_{ui}^* \neq B_{ui})$ abort		
Else ask for identity and password		
Input (ID_{ui}^*, PW_{ui})		
Compute $e_{ui}^* = h(ID_{ui}||PW_{ui}||B_{ui})$		
if $(e_{ui}^* \neq e_{ui})$ abort		
Else, compute $d_i^* = f_i \oplus h(ID_{ui}^*||PW_{ui}^*)$		
Compute $L_i^* = g_{ui} \oplus h(PW_{ui}^* \oplus ID_{ui}^*)$		
Generate r_i and T_1		
Compute $M_1 = ID_{ui}^* \oplus h(L_i^*||T_1)$		
Compute $M_2 = r_i \oplus h(d_i^*||T_i$		
Compute $M_3 = h(d_i^*||r_i||T_1)$		
Compute $SCT_x = SCN_j \oplus h(T_1)$		
Chose ID_{ui}		
$EID_{SN} = ID_{SN} \oplus h(ID_{ui}||r_i||T_1)$		
$\xrightarrow{MSG_1=\{M_1,M_2,M_3,T_1,SCT_i,EID_{SN}\}}$		
(unreliable channel)		
	Compute $SCN = SCT_x \oplus h(T_1)$	
	Compute $L_i' = h(SCN||X_{GN})$	
	Compute $ID_{ui} = M_1 \oplus h(L_i'||T_1)$	
	Compute $d_i' = h(ID_{ui}'||X_{GN})$	
	Compute $r_i' = M_2 \oplus h(d_i'||T_1)$	
	Compute $M_3 = h(d_i'||r_i'||T_1)$	
	if $(M_3' \neq M_3)$, abort	
	Else, Compute $M_4 = h(ID_{ui}||d_i'||T_1)$	
	$\xleftarrow{MSG_2=(M_4)}$	
	unreliable channel	
Compute $M_4^* = h(ID_{ui}||d_i^*||T_1)$		
if $(M_4^* \neq M_4)$, abort		
Else compute $M_5 = h(d_i^*||ID_{ui}||r_i||T_1)$		
$\xrightarrow{MSG_3=(M_5)}$		
unreliable channel		
	Compute $M_5' = h(d_i'||ID_{ui}'||r_i'||T_1)$	
	if $(M_5' \neq M_5)$, abort	
	Else,compute $ID_{SN}' = EID_{SN} \oplus h(ID_{ui}||r_i||T_1)$	
	Compute $X_{SN}' = h(ID_{SN}'||X_{GN})$	
	$M_6 = h(ID_{ui}'||ID_{SN}'||ID_{GN}||X_{SN}'||r_i'||T_2)$	
	Compute $M_7 = ID' \oplus h(ID_{GN}||X_{SN}'||T_2)$	
	Compute $M_8 = r_i \oplus h(ID_{ui}'||X_{SN}')$	
	$\xrightarrow{MSG_4=\{ID_{GN},M_6,M_7,M_8,T_2\}}$	
	unreliable channel	
		If $\mid T_3 - T_2 \mid \leq \triangle T$ is false
		Else, compute $ID_{ui}^{**} = M_7 \oplus h(ID_{GN}||X_{SN}||T_2)$
		$r_i^{**} = M_8 \oplus h(ID_{ui}^{**}||X_{SN})$
		$M_6^{**} = h(ID_{ui}^{**}||ID_{SN}||ID_{GN}||X_{SN}||r_i^{**}||T_2)$
		if $(M_6^{**} \neq M_6)$, abort
		$SK_{SN} = h(ID_{ui}^{**}||ID_{SN}||r_i^{**}||r_s)$
		Compute $M_9 = h(SK_{SN}||S_{SN}||r_s||T_3)$
		Compute $M_{10} = r_i^{**} \oplus r_s$
		$\xleftarrow{MSG_5=(M_9,M_{10},T_3)}$
	If $\mid T_4 - T_3 \mid \leq \triangle T$ is false, abort	
	Else compute $r_s' = M_{10} \oplus r_i$	
	Compute $SK_{GN} = h(ID_{ui}'||ID_{ui}||r_i'||r_s')$	
	Compute $M_9' = SK_{GN}||X_{SN}'||r_i'||T_3$	
	if $(M_9' \neq M_9)$, abort	
	Else Compute $M_{11} = h(SK_{GN}||ID_{ui}'||d_i||r_s')$	
	$\xleftarrow{MSG_6=(M_{11},M_{10})}$	
Compute $r_s^* = M_{10} \oplus r_i$		
$SK_{ui} = h(ID_{ui}||ID_{SN}||r_i||r_s^*)$		
$M_{11}^* = h(SK_{ui}||ID_{ui}||d_i||r_s)$		
if $(M_{11}^* \neq M_{11})$, abort		
Else, accept GN and SN		

Figure 2.3: Login and authentication phase in [1] scheme

In Amin et al.'s protocol, the SCT_x is transmitted over the open channel so, when a legal users sends more than one login request with the same ID the adversary $\mathcal{A}$ can easily trace the initiator/user with SCT_x and trace out the user of the system which is clear violation of anonymity. Thus this problem may also lead to user traceability. Whereas, $SCT_x = SCN \oplus h(T_x)$.

2.3 Problem Statement

In recent past researchers developed many authentication protocols for user authentication and security vulnerabilities in WSN and IOT environment. Furthermore, these schemes [1,2,5,30] respectively are efficient to overcome some security problems related to user authentication and agreement of the session key in WSN, but still these previous schemes are vulnerable to many security attacks. Most recently Amin et al.[1] find out various security limitations of the Farash et al.[30] protocol and they extended the same protocol to improve its security weaknesses and claimed that the protocol is secure in all aspects. In this thesis we scrutinized the Amin et al. protocol which reveals that the protocol still having the following numerous security weaknesses:-

1. Traceability attack.

2. User anonymity

2.4 Chapter Summary

In WSN major issue is authenticity of message via a communication channel between the two parties to establish the exchange of data in safe way. In the aforementioned literature many protocols of WSN authentication were discussed by different researcher like password/pin code base authentication, two factor authentication but these schemes still having some issues of security. A Biometric based authentication were designed for the solution of the same problems because biometric keys are hard to steal, allocate, distribute and share. Biometrics based authentications are hard to guessed, steel and also not breakdown easily. In this chapter we discussed some related schemes of different researchers with their importance and limitations. In the last section of this chapter we stated the problem statement of our thesis.

Chapter 3

Proposed Solution

In this chapter, we explain the novel enhanced protocol which based totally on the flaws of Amin et al.'s scheme. The addendum scheme is not just forceful against all identified attacks but in addition conserved the innovative merits of the protocol of Amin et al.'s. The main identified loopholes of [1] is highlighted in registration phase and login and authen-tication phase of our proposed protocol. The key flaws of Amin et al.'s protocol is violation of user anony-mity and user traceability attack. Our proposed scheme based on symmetric cryptography due to constraint resources of WSN, we use three factor authentication to improve the Amin et al.'s protocol. We used simple encryption/decryption with simple hash function, XOR operation and biometric extraction function $BK()$ for biometric features extraction. The proposed anonymous scheme resist against all possible attack and problem that are examined in[1] complete security analysis are given in chapter 4 of the thesis. Previous scheme were also based on three factor authentication but with non provision of anonymity. Our scheme is principally consisting of three participant entities i.e. user, sensor node and gateway node and comprising of nine phases which have been discussed in this subsection below.

3.1   System Setup Phase

The System Setup phase is actually configure in offline mode by the by the System Adminis-trator SA. Description of this phase are as under:-

Step 1: SA selects the identity ID_{SN} of the sensor node of $SN(1 \leq j \leq m)$

Step 2: System Administrator chose a master key X_{GN} this key only known to GN, then computes $X_{SN} = h(ID_{SN}||X_{GN})$, X_{SN} which is the secret key of SN which is unique for each SN.

Step 3: The System Administrator SA chose a random number R_{shrd} between the GN and SN. Finally SA push $\{ID_{SN}, X_{SN}, R_{shrd}\}$ in the temper memory of SN in safe way. So we imagine that adversary $\mathcal{A}$ not extract $\{ID_{SN}, X_{SN}, R_{shrd}\}$ for the SN memory even if compromise.

3.2   Registration Phase of the Sensor Node

After the system setup phase the SA deploy the sensor node SN with a single GN on the target region and make a sensor network. This phase is illustrated in figure 3.1. In registration of the Sensor node SN every sensor-node SN carry out the underneath step with GN.

Step 1: A SN computes B_1 and B_2, $B_1 = ID_{SN} \oplus h(R_{shrd}||T_1)$, $B_2 = h(ID_{SN}||B_{SN}||R_{shrd}||T_1)$ then send B_1 and B_2 with timestamp T_{s1} via an unreliable channel to GN where T_{s1} is a new timestamps.

Step 2: GN verify these parameters with timestamp $\mid T_{GN} - T_{s1} \mid \leq \triangle T$ hold. If incorrect the SN reject GN, otherwise computing $ID'_{SN} = B_1 \oplus h(R_{shrd} \parallel T_{s1})$, $X_{SN} = h(ID'_{SN}||X_{GN})$, and $B'_2 = h(ID'_{SN} \parallel B'_{SN} \parallel R_{shrd} \parallel T_{s1})$ to check whether $B'_2 = B_2$ holds. If false the GN reject the SN. Otherwise SN are authenticates by GN and stored ID_{SN} in memory.

Step 3: After the registration phase the confirmation message send to SN by GN after successful completion of registration and R_{shrd} are deleted by SN from memory.

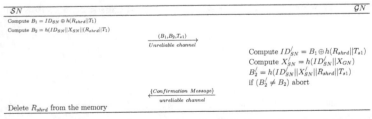

Figure 3.1: Sensor node registration phase of proposed scheme

3.3   User Registration Phase

This phase is shown in figure 3.2 also their steps are describe below:-

Step 1: The user U_i select an identity ID_{ui} and send this identity alongwith personal record via a reliable channel to SA, personal record assist in re-issuing of fresh smart-card for those U_i whose smart-card are lost, stolen or damage by some reasons.

Step 2: If the System Administrator SA found this ID_{ui} in database if exist, it request for fresh ID_{ui} ; otherwise compute $d_i = h(ID_{ui}||X_{GN})$ and $L_i = h(SCN||X_{GN})$. Here in the previous scheme [1] the SCN is transmitted in plain text over the public channel but in proposed scheme we encrypted the same with secret key of X_{GN} compute as $SCN_j = E_{X_{GN}}(SCN||r_0)$ then store these parameters in the Smart-card $\{d_i, L_i, SCN_j, BK()\}$ and send it to user through reliable channel.At this point $BK()$ represent the biometric key creation and extraction function. The SA also keep up a table in which storing ID_{ui} and the personal documentation of every user U_i.

Step 3: U_i put in the smart-card in the card-reader. U_i enter (ID_{ui}, PW_{ui}) and fingerprint fng_{ui} through sensor device to smart-card. Then the smart-card compute $B_{ui} = BK(H(fng_{ui})), e_{ui} = h(ID_{ui}||PW_{ui}||B_{ui}), f_{ui} = d_i \oplus h(ID_{ui}||PW_{ui})$ and $g_{ui} = L_i \oplus h(PW_{ui} \oplus ID_{ui})$, here H(.)   is a bio-hashing function. Smart-card store $\{ B_{ui}, e_{ui}, f_{ui}, g_{ui}, SCN_j, BK()\}$ in its memory and deleted (d_i, l_i).

3.4   Login Phase

In our login phase when the register user want to get the real time sensor information, they execute some steps of this login message, sending these information to GN via an unreliable way The details of this phase are specified in figure 3.3 and underneath:-

Step 1: U_i put the smart-card into the card reader and captured fingerprint fng_{ui} through sensor device. Then these parameters are computed by smart-card: $B_{ui}^* = BK(H(fng_{ui}))$, also check where $B_{ui}^* = B_{ui}$. If this verification is false, then the smart-card reject the login request of U_i's otherwise ask for identity password. The U_i given ID_{ui} and PW_{ui} to smart-card so it computes $e_{ui}^* = h(ID_{ui} \parallel PW_{ui} \parallel B_{ui})$ the smartcard abort the session if, if $e_{ui}^* \neq e_{ui}$ otherwise, $ID_{ui}^* = ID_{ui}$ and $PW_{ui}^* = PW_{ui}$ hold.

Step 2: After verification & checking the genuineness of U_i then, the same smart-card computes $d_{ui}^* = f_{ui} \oplus h(ID_{ui}^* \parallel PW_{ui}^*)$ and $L_i^* = g_{ui} \oplus h(PW_{ui}^* \oplus ID_{ui}^*)$. The Smart-card

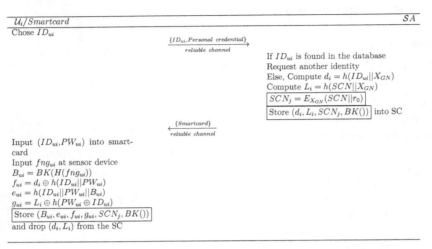

Figure 3.2: User Registration Phase of Proposed Scheme

also generate timestamp T_1 and random number r_i to computes: $M_1 = ID_{ui}^* \oplus h(L_i^*||T_1)$, $M_2 = r_i \oplus h(d_i^*||T_1)$, $M_3 = h(d_i^* \parallel r_i \parallel T_1)$ and $SCT_x = SCN_j \oplus h(T_1)$. The smart-card demand from the user U_i for the identity of the sensor-node ID_{SN}. Th user chosen the sensor node SN and entered its identity in the memory of the smart-card.

Step 3: In this step the Smart-card calculates $EID_{SN} = ID_{SN} \oplus h(ID_{ui}||r_i||T_1)$ and send $MSG_1 = (M_1, M_2, M_3, T_1, SCT_x, EID_{SN})$ to GN using an unreliable channel.

3.5 Authentication and Session Key Agreement Phase

In the subject phase mutual authentication as well as session key agreement are executed between U_i, GN and SN the detail of this phase is illustrated in figure 3.3.

Step 1: After the receiving of login message MSG_1 by GN from U_i then GN computes $SCN_j = SCT_x \oplus h(T_1)$, decrypt SCN_j as $(SCN||r_0) = D_{X_{GN}}(SCN_j)$ and computes $L_i^/ = h(SCN \parallel X_{GN})$, $ID_{ui}^/ = M_1 \oplus h(L_i^/ \parallel T_1)$, $d_i^/ = h(ID_{ui}^/ \parallel X_{GN})$, $r_i^/ = M_2 \oplus h(d_i^/ \parallel T_1)$ and $M_3^/ = h(d_i^/ \parallel r_i^/ \parallel T_1)$. The GN abort the session if $M_3^/ \neq M_3$. Otherwise compute $M_4 = h(ID_{ui} \parallel d_i^/ \parallel T_1)$ and encrypted the unique smart-card number with the secret key of GN. So as the $SCN_{jnew} = E_{X_{GN}}(SCN||r_0)$, compute $M_5 = SCN_{jnew} \oplus L_i$

and send $MSG_2 = (M_4, M_5)$ using an unreliable channel to user U_i.

Step 2: The U_i received the message MSG_2 and computes $M_4^* = h(ID_{ui} \parallel d_i^* \parallel T_1)$, so this session is abort by U_i if M_4^* is not equal to M_4 otherwise it computing $M_6 = h(d_i^* \parallel ID_{ui} \parallel r_i \parallel T_1)$, $SCN_j = M_5 \oplus L_i$ and send $MSG_3 = (M_6, SCN_j)$ via an unreliable channel to GN.

Step 3: The GN received M_3 from U_i and computes $M_6^{/} = h(d_i^{/} \parallel ID_{ui}^{/} \parallel r_i^{/} \parallel T_1)$, the same session will be abort if $M_6^{/} \neq M_6$, otherwise it assured that the attacker does not lunch any reply attack.

Step 4: In order to check legitimacy of U_i, GN to SN, GN compute $ID_{SN}^{/} = EID_{SN} \oplus h(ID_{ui} \parallel r_i \parallel T_1)$, $X_{SN}^{/} = h(ID_{ui}^{/} \parallel X_{GN})$, $M_7 = h(ID_{ui}^{/} \parallel ID_{SN}^{/} \parallel ID_{GN} \parallel X_{SN}^{/} \parallel r_i^{/} \parallel T_2)$, $M_8 = ID^{/} \oplus h(ID_{GN} \parallel X_{SN}^{/} \parallel T_2)$ and $M_9 = r_i \oplus h(ID_{ui}^{/} \parallel X_{SN}^{/})$ and send $MSG_4 = \{ID_{GN}, M_7, M_8, M_9, T_2\}$ via an unreliable channel to SN.

Step 5: SN check true timestamp $\mid T_3 - T_2 \mid \leq \Delta T$ holds, if it is false SN immediately terminate the session otherwise compute: $ID_{ui}^{**} = M_8 \oplus h(ID_{GN} \parallel X_{SN} \parallel T_2)$, $r_{ui}^{**} = M_9 \oplus h(ID_{ui}^{**} \parallel X_{SN})$ and $M_7^{**} = h(ID_{ui}^{**} \parallel ID_{SN} \parallel ID_{GN} \parallel X_{SN} \parallel r_i^{**} \parallel T_2)$, SN also abort the connection if $M_7^{**} \neq M_7$, otherwise compute: $SK_{SN} = h(ID_{ui}^{**} \parallel ID_{SN} \parallel r_i^{**} \parallel r_s)$, $M_{10} = h(SK_{SN} \parallel X_{SN} \parallel r_s \parallel T_3)$ and $M_{11} = (r_i^{**} \oplus r_s)$ and send $MSG_5 = \{M_{10}, M_{11}, T_3\}$ to GN via an unreliable channel.

Step 6: GN check the timestamp T_4 which is current timestamp or not if it is false the GN eliminate the session, otherwise it compute: $r_s^{/} = M_{10} \oplus r_i$, $SK_{GN} = h(ID_{ui}^{/} \parallel ID_{SN} \parallel r_i^{/} \parallel r_s^{/})$ and $M_{10}^{/} = h(SK_{GN} \parallel X_{SN}^{/} \parallel r_s^{/} \parallel T_3)$, GN abort the session if $M_{10}^{/}$ is not equal to M_{10}, otherwise compute $M_{12} = h(SK_{GN} \parallel ID_{ui}^{/} \parallel d_i \parallel r_s^{/})$ and send $MSG_6 = \{M_{12}, M_{11}\}$ via an unreliable channel to U_i.

Step 7: U_i computes $r_s^* = M_{12} \oplus r_i$, $SK_{ui} = h(ID_{ui} \parallel ID_{SN} \parallel r_i \parallel r_s^*)$, $M_{12}^* = h(SK_{ui} \parallel ID_{ui} \parallel d_i \parallel r_s)$ so abort the session if $M_{12}^* \neq M_{12}$ otherwise U_i believe on authenticity between GN and SN. This protocol then establish session key $SK_{ui} = SK_{SN} = SK_{GN}$ between U_i, SN and GN after mutual authentication. The main purpose of this scheme in this phase is the negotiation of the session key $SK_{ui} = SK_{SN} = SK_{GN}$ among the above three main entities.

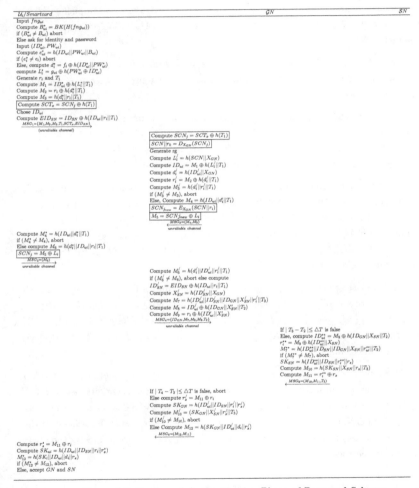

Figure 3.3: Login and Authentication Phase of Proposed Scheme

3.6 Post Deployment Phase

The key purpose of post deployment phase is the deployment of sensor-nodes later the accomplishment of the sensor network. There is a practical issue in this phase when one or many sensor node becomes damaged so requisite replacement of the same is necessary. Suppose that a damage node SN_d require to be change with fresh sensor node SN_f in the target area. The SA choses the identity ID_f of SN_f to do so, and computes $X_f = h(ID_f||X_{GN})$, and insert (ID_f, X_f, R_{shrd}) in memory of SN_f. Now, SA deploys SN_f on the target field. After deployment the SN_f computes the registration phase of the sensor node as represent in figure in the previous section.

3.7 Identity Update Phase

The main purpose of the above subject phase is the enhancement of security to updates the identity of the register user with the assistance of GN. U_i enter the smart-card in the card-reader and computes the step 1 of the proposed login phase to confirm U_i authenticity. Now the Smart-card and U_i performed the underneath steps:-

Step 1: When U_i insert the new identity ID_{ui}^{new} so as the smart-card Calculate: $d_i^* = f_{ui} \oplus h(ID_{ui}||PW_{ui}), L_i^* = g_{ui} \oplus h(PW_{ui} \oplus ID_{ui}), Z_i = h(d_i^*||ID_{ui}||T_{id}), W_{ui} = ID_{ui} \oplus h(L_i||d_i||T_{id}), SCT_x = SCN_j \oplus h(T_{id})$ and $ID_{ui} = ID_{ui}^{new} \oplus h(L_i||d_i||T_{id})$. Then the smart-card deliver these $\{Z_i, W_{ui}, ID_{ui}, SCT_j, T_{id}\}$ to GN via unreliable channel.

Step 2: Then on the other hand GN computes $SCN_j = SCT_x \oplus h(T_{id}), L_i^/ = h(SCN||X_{GN}), ID_{ui}^/ = W_{ui} \oplus h(L_i^/||T_{id}), d_i^/ = d_i^/ = h(ID_{ui}^/||X_{GN})$ and $Z_i^/ = Z_i$ hold, then if true then GN computes: $ID_{ui}^{new} = ID_{ui} \oplus h(L_i^/||d_i^/||T_{id}), d_i^{**} = h(ID_{ui}^{new}||X_{GN}), Y_{ui} = d_i^{**} \oplus d_i^/$ and $ZZ_i = h(d_i^{**}||Z_i^/)$ and send (ZZ_i, Y_{ui}) to smart-card via an unreliable channel, and also updates new Id in Database.

Step 3: In this step smart-computes $d_i^{**} = Y_{ui} \oplus d_i^/, ZZ_i^* = h(d_i^*||Z_i)$ and checks $ZZ_i^* = ZZ_i$ holds, if this condition is true then smart-card computes $e_i^{new} = h(ID_{ui}^{new}||PW_{ui}||B_{ui}), f^{new_{ui}} = d_i^{**} \oplus h(ID_{ui}^{new}||PW_{ui})$ and $g_{ui}^{new} = L_i \oplus h(PW_{ui} \oplus ID_{ui}^{new})$, lastly the old information are replace by smart-card $\{e_{ui}, f_{ui}, g_{ui}\}$ with new information $\{e_{ui}^{new}, f^{new_{ui}}, g_{ui}^{new}\}$ and store the same parameter on the smart-card.

3.8 Password Change Phase

In password based authentication protocol must include password modification the concerned user U_i any time change their password for the enhancement of security without the assistance of SA or GN. The detail specification of this phase is narrated as under:-

Step 1: U_i entered the smart-card within the card-reader and re-process step 1 of the login phase checked the legitimacy of identity, password and fingerprints.

Step 2: The Smart-card insist U_i for a fresh password, PW_{ui}^{new}, U_i insert fresh password PW_{ui}^{new} then smart-card Calculate $e_{ui}^{new}h(ID_{ui}||PW_{ui}^{new}||B_{ui})$, $d_i' = f_{ui}\oplus h(ID_{ui}||PW_{ui})$, $f_{ui}^{new} = d_i^{new} \oplus h(ID_{ui}||PW_{ui}^{new})$, $L_i' = g_i \oplus h(PW_{ui} \oplus ID_{ui})$ and $g_{ui}^{new} = L_i' \oplus h(PW_{ui}^{new} \oplus ID_{ui})$.

Step 3: Smart-card update the old record (e_{ui}, g_{ui}, f_{ui}) with new $\{e_{ui}^{new}, g_{ui}^{new}, f_{ui}^{new}\}$ in smart-card memory. The other factors remain unchanged.

3.9 Smart-card Revocation Phase

In the practical issue when the register user U_i of the network smart-card is misplace or stolen so in this protocol user obtained the new smart-card with the computation of the following steps.

Step 1: U_i send his/her identity ID_{ui} alongwith personal information to the SA via a reliable channel. SA verify U_i personal credentials of the user if valid then computes: $d_i^{new} = h(ID_{ui}||X_{GN})$ and $L_i^{new} = h(SCN^{new}||X_{GN})$, SCN^{new} is a unique number of new smart-card. The SA keeps $\{d_i^{new}, L_i^{new}, SCN^{new}, BK()\}$ in the new smart-card memory and send it securely to user. SA modify the Database with SCN^{new}.

Step 2: U_i enter the new smart-card in the card-reader and entered the identity ID_{ui}, password PW_{ui} and fingerprint fng_{ui} with fingerprint device and computes: $B_{ui}^{new} = BK(H(fng_{ui}))$, $e_{ui}^{new} = h(ID_{ui}||PW_{ui}||B_{ui}^{new})$, $f_{ui}^{new} = d_i^{new} \oplus h(ID_{ui}||PW_{ui})$ and $g_{ui}^{new} = L_i^{new} \oplus h(PW_{ui} \oplus ID_{ui})$. Finally Smart-card store $(B_{ui}^{new}, e_{ui}^{new}, f_{ui}^{new}, g_{ui}^{new}, SCN_j^{new}, BK())$ in its memory and delete $\{d_i^{new} L_i^{new}\}$ from memory.

3.10 Chapter Summary

We presented the features of proposed protocol in this chapter with their significant nine phases to avoid the user anonymity and traceablity attack which has already been discussed in cryptanalysis in chapter 2. In this chapter, we also present the dealings to avoid all possible attacks and make the user hidden (anonymous) on the same protocol. In the cryptanalysis we have already examined and declare the two categories of threats and user anonymity breach of the R. Amin et al. protocol. After that we presented several principles for safety of the protocols. We also presented some approaches for scheming the security protocols and then we tried to improve the protocol with the procedures offered. Numeral examples in the literature have also been made known that the work completed in the document is especially momentous.

Chapter 4

Security Analysis

In this chapter we evaluate and examine the safety features and robustness of the intended improved authentication protocol. We are considering this security measurement in the light of adversarial model which we discussed in chapter 1. Moreover in the next subsection we examined that the proposed protocol is strong/healthy against all possible attacks of the adversary or not. In addition, described the comparison and security requirements of proposed protocol. Since, considerate thoughts of cryptographic protocols required so that we are capable to observe the information about protocol contestants and challenger. Upon receiving a message by the opponents:-

1. Does he/she identify that who sends it?

2. Does he/she recognize that the message is fresh?

3. Does he/she know that it is never just a repetition of something from the past message?

4. Does the system investigator identify who is communicating to whom?

The security analysis of the proposed protocol can be divided into two categories formally and informally.

4.1 Formal Security Analysis

In web technology communication not only share the information among the entities but they have some rules for their communication which known as protocols. So the security of these protocols is very important for the secure sharing of information. In any regulations manipulating, cryptographic functions also desirable for several explicit problems solution within a protocol. The proper security examination of the novel protocol has been verified by using ProVerif and BAN logic.

4.1.1 Security Analysis with BAN logic

In this part we presented the authentication of our proposed scheme through proper security examination by using a tool BAN-Logic. This tool was first published in 1989 by Burrows, Abadi and Needham. This was the first idea for the inspection and descriptions of authentication schemes. It is a valuable tool that expresses the impression of truthful parties engaged in the communication as well progression of these trusts as a outcome of communication. The conservative technique for the description of these protocols, by catalog the destination, source and contents symbolically, is change with logical principle. This representation goal to prepare the protocol all steps in a method that all the necessary information expand from the step is revealed. This is known as idealization of the procedure. Additionally, the idealized protocol is interpreted with declaration, which typically describes the beliefs of the rule at that spot of the protocol. At the similar time the protocol is investigate step by step using some set of assumption rules [31].

There are some special notations use for BAN Logic for the description of the logic, suppose sign P and Q denote the principals X and Y are the sort over the declaration and K be the Cryptography key. The most frequently used concepts and some symbol of BAN-Logic, are describe as under:-

Table 4.1: Notations and Concepts in BAN-Logic

Notations	Description
$P \mid \equiv Q$	P believes Q
$P \triangleleft Q$	P sees Q
$P \mid \sim Q$	P said Q once
$P \Rightarrow Q$	P has jurisdiction on Q
$\#(X)$	X is fresh
(X, Y)	X or Y are piece of principle (X,Y)
$< X >_Y$	The X rule is joined with Y
$\{X\}_K$	This show that formula X is encoded with key K
$(X)_K$	This show that X value hashed with the key K
$P \xleftrightarrow{K} Q$	P and Q are shared Private key K
$P \xrightarrow{K} Q$	P have a public key K
SK	SK Session Key

4.1.2   Rules of BAN-Logic

Burrows, Abadi and Needham were define varies rules for the authentication of protocols. As per these defined rule if only one rule violate, then that protocol should be understood erroneous one. The descriptions of these rules are as under:-

Principals: Those individuals who are concerned in the protocol (typically people or plans).

Keys: It use for encryption of messages symmetrically.

Public Keys: It is also a key but it used in a pairs.

Nonces: It is a random numbers or part of messages which are not repeated.

Timestamps: It is the recent time of a happening that are unluckily to be repetitive.

Rule 1: Message Meaning

$$\frac{P|\equiv P \xleftarrow{K} Q. P \triangleleft <X>_K}{P|\equiv Q|\sim X}$$

It shows that if P obtain the X encoded with Key K and P deems K is fine key to communicate with Q, and then P believes Q said X.

Rule 2: Nonce Verification

$$\frac{P|\equiv\#(X), P|\equiv Q|\sim X}{P|\equiv Q|\equiv X}$$

When a principal P trusted that X is new/fresh also then principal Q only once time sends X after that Principal after that P believe Q held X.

Rule 3: Jurisdiction

$$\frac{P|\equiv Q \Rightarrow X, P|\equiv Q|\equiv X}{P|\equiv X}$$

Principal P believes that Q have control/jurisdiction on X also P believes that Q believes X, after that P trusted that X is right.

Rule 4: Acceptance Conjuncatenation

$$\frac{P|\equiv X, P|\equiv Y}{P|\equiv(X,Y)}$$

If a principal P is believes X as well as Y, subsequently then principal P also believes on (X, Y).

Rule 5: Freshness Conjuncatenation

$$\frac{P|\equiv\#(X)}{P|\equiv\#(X,Y)}$$

If a principal P confident that X is a fresh, after that a principal P also believes newness / freshness of (X, Y).

Rule 6: Session Key

$$\frac{P|\equiv\#(X),P|\equiv Q\equiv X}{P|\equiv\ P\xleftrightarrow{K}Q}$$

If a principal P believe the fresh session key also then principal P as well 'Q' also believes on X which is the essential constraint of a session key, next principal P also believes that he/she share a session key 'K' with Q.

4.1.3 BAN Logic Procedure for Protocol Analysis

To institute proposed protocol is safe, the given procedure should be exercised.

- In the first step idealize the planned authentication protocol in a formal logic of the language.

- In the second step recognize the assumption regarding the preliminary state of proposed authentication protocol.

- In third step utilize the production and utilize the rule of a logic to infer new predicates.

- In fourth step use the logic to find out the beliefs apprehended by the entities within the proposed proposal.

In order to verify the proposed scheme safe, the proposed scheme be required to satisfy the below goals which depend on the mechanism of BAN-Logic which are specified as under:-

- G1: $GN|\equiv U_i \xleftrightarrow{SK}$ GN

- G2: $GN| \equiv U_i| \equiv U_i \overset{SK}{\longleftrightarrow} GN$

- G3: $SN| \equiv GN \overset{SK}{\longleftrightarrow} SN$

- G4: $SN| \equiv GN| \equiv GN \overset{SK}{\longleftrightarrow} SN$

- G5: $GN| \equiv SN \overset{SK}{\longleftrightarrow} GN$

- G6: $GN| \equiv SN| \equiv SN \overset{SK}{\longleftrightarrow} GN$

- G7: $U_i| \equiv GN \overset{SK}{\longleftrightarrow} U_i$

- G8: $U_i| \equiv GN| \equiv GN \overset{SK}{\longleftrightarrow} U_i$

Part1: The proposed protocol Idealized form are as under:-

- M1: $U_i \to GN: M_1 : M_2 :< d_i^* > r_i,\ M_3 < d_i^* > r_i,\ SCT_x, EID_{SN}, T_1$

- M2: $GN \to U_i: M_4 < d_i >$

- M3: $U_i \to GN : M_6 < d_i^* > r_i$

- M4: $GN \to SN : ID_{SN}, M_6 :< r_i > X_{SN}, M_7,\ M_8 :< r_i > X_{SN}$

- M5: $SN \to GN: M_9 < SKsn > SN: M_{10} :< r_i > r_s, T_3$

- M6: $SN \to U_i: M_{11} :< d_i > r_s, M_{12} :< r_i^{**} > r_s$

Part2: Assumptions for analysis the protocol are as under:-

- A1: $U_i| \equiv \#(r_i, r_s)$

- A2: $GN| \equiv \#(r_i), GN| \equiv \#(r_s)$

- A3: $SN| \equiv \#(r_i, r_s)$

- B1: $GN| \equiv U_i \Rightarrow r_i$

- B2: $GN| \equiv SN \Rightarrow r_s$

- B3: $SN| \equiv U_i \Rightarrow r_i$

- B4: $U_i| \equiv SN \Rightarrow r_s$

- C1: $U_i| \equiv U_i \overset{SCN_j}{\longleftrightarrow} GN$

- C2: $GN| \equiv GN \overset{X_{SN}}{\longleftrightarrow} SN$

- C3: $SN| \equiv SN \overset{X_{SN}}{\longleftrightarrow} SN$

- C4: $GN| \equiv GN \overset{d_i}{\longleftrightarrow} Ui$

Part3: Analysis based on Assumptions and BAN Logic Rules which is stated as under:-

MSG1: $U_i \rightarrow GN$: $M_1 : M_2 :< d_i^* > r_i$, $M_3 < d_i^* > r_i$, SCT_x, EID_{SN}, T_1

According to seeing Rules we get:

- S1: $GN \triangleleft M_1 : M_2 < d_i^* > r_i : M_3 < d_i^* > r_i, SCT_x, EID_{SN}, T_1$

By Applying C1 message meaning Rules and S1 we obtain:

- S2:$GN |\equiv U_i |\sim r_i$

According to Assumption A2,freshness conjuncatenation Rules, nonce verification Rules and S2 we obtain:

- S3:$GN |\equiv U_i |\equiv r_i$

By applying jurisdiction Rule according to B1 and S3, we get:

- S4:$GN |\equiv r_i$

As per assumption A2, S3 and by applying session key Rules we obtain:

- S5:$GN |\equiv U_i \xleftrightarrow{SK} GN$ (**Goal1**)

By applying nonce verification law and assumption A2 and S5 we obtain:

- $GN |\equiv U_i \equiv U_i \xleftrightarrow{SK} GN$ (**Goal2**)

MSG4: $GN \rightarrow SN$: $M_6 : M_2 :< r_1' > X_{SN}$, M_7,$M8 :< r_i' > X_{SN}$

As per seeing Rule we discover:

- S7:$SN \triangleleft M_6 < r_i' > X_{SN}$,$M_7$,$M8 :< r_i > X_{SN}$

As per S7 and message meaning rules we find:

- S8:$SN |\equiv GN |\sim r_g$

- S9:$SN |\equiv GN |\equiv r_g$

- S10:$SN |\equiv r_g$

- S11:$SN |\equiv GN |\xleftrightarrow{SK} SN$ (**Goal3**)

- S12:$SN |\equiv GN |\equiv GN \xleftrightarrow{SK} SN$ (**Goal4**)

MSG5: $SN \rightarrow GN$: $M_9 < SK_{SN} >$, $M_{10} < r_i^{**} > r_s$,T3

Applying seeing Rule

- S13:$GN \triangleleft M_9 < SK_{SN} > SN$,$M_{10} < r_i^{**} > r_s$,T3

According to A2, S3 and by applying message-meaning Conduct we discover:

- S14: $GN| \equiv SN| \sim r_s$

According to C3 and freshness-conjuncatenation Rules we find:

- S15: $GN| \equiv SN| \equiv r_s$

By applying jurisdiction Rule and assumption A2 we find:

- S16: $GN| \equiv r_s$

As per A2, S15 and session key Rules we obtain:

- S17: $GN| \equiv SN| \xleftrightarrow{SK} GN$ (**Goal5**)

By applying nonce verification Rule and with assumption A2 and S17 we get.

- $GN| \equiv SN| \equiv SN \xleftrightarrow{SK} GN$ (**Goal6**)

MSG6: $GN \to U_i$: $M_{11} < d_i > r'_s$, $M_{10} < r_i^{**} > r_s$
By applying seeing Rule we get.

- S18: $U_i \lhd M_{11} < d_i > r'_s, M_{10} < r_i^{**} > r_s$

Applying A2, S18 and message-meaning Rule we obtain.

- S19: $U_i| \equiv GN| \sim r_g$

According to C4, S19 and freshness Rule we get.

- S20: $U_i| \equiv GN| \equiv r'_g$

By applying A2, S20 and Jurisdiction Rule we get.

- S21: $U_i| \equiv r'_g$

By applying session key Rule and S21 we get:

- S22: $U_i| \equiv GN| \xleftrightarrow{SK} U_i$ (**Goal7**)

The nonce verification Rule and assumption A2, S7 we get:

- $U_i| \equiv GN| \equiv GN \xleftrightarrow{SK} U_i$ (**Goal8**)

The proposed scheme make sure by using the verification tool BAN Logic which show that all the three participant entities U_i, GN and SN successfully achieve the session key agreement and mutual authentication.

4.1.4 ProVerif

ProVerif is verification tool which use for assessment and robustness of the protocols against all possible active attack. The same tool kit is also examine the insider attack which known some cryptographic parameters. This verification tool analyzes the protocol against strong adversaries attacks from all angles. ProVerif can verify various security elements, for example: traceability, anonymity, reachability, secrecy and authentication [14]. ProVerif is based on pi calculus which uses logical and arithmetic procedure. ProVerif tool having the given three elements: declaration, process also main part. The first part is used for defining variable cryptographic primal and contents. As illustrated in the figure, we actually define tow channel private and public.

```
(***--------- Channels --------***)
free ChSec:channel [private]. (***secure channel between UI and SN***)
free ChPub:channel ...  (**public channel between UI,GN and SN**)
(*********Constants and Variables**********)
free IDui :bitstring.
free IDGN :bitstring.
free IDsn :bitstring.
free PWui : bitstring [private]..
free Xsn :bitstring [private]..
free ri :bitstring [private]..
free XGN:bitstring [private]..
free SCN:bitstring [private]..
(*========Constructors=======*)
fun h(bitstrings):bitstrings..
fun Inverse(bitstrings):bitstrings.
fun Concat(bitstrings,bitstrings):bitstrings..
fun XOR(bitstrings,bitstring):bitstrings..
fun Mult(bitstrings,bitstrings):bitstrings..
fun enc(bitstrings, bitstrings): bitstrings..
fun dec(bitstrings ,bitstrings): bitstrings..

(*=====Equations======*)
```

```
equation forall a:bitstrings; Inverse(Inverse(a))=a.
equation for all a:bitstrings, b:bitstrings; XOR(XOR(a,b),b)=a.
equation for all x: bitstrings, y: bitstrings; dec(enc(x,y),y) = x.
equation for all x: bitstrings, y: bitstrings; enc(dec(x,y),y) = x.
(*-------queries------*)
free SK:bitstrings [private].
query attacker(SK).
query id:bitstrings; inj-event(end_UI(IDui)) ==> inj-event(start_UI(IDui)).
query id:bitstrings; inj-event(end_GN(IDGN)) ==> inj-event(start_GN(IDGN)).
query id:bitstrings; inj-event(end_SN(IDsn)) ==> inj-event(start_SN(IDsn)).
(*======*Events*======*)
event start_UI(bitstrings).
event end_UI(bitstrings).
event start_GN(bitstrings).
event end_GN(bitstrings).
event start_SN(bitstrings).
event end_SN(bitstrings).
let  pUI=
(*****************Registration phase*****************)
out(ChSec,(IDui));
in (ChSec,(Li:bitstring,di:bitstring,BK:bitstring));
new fngi: bitstring;
let Bui = Mult(BK,(h(fngui))) in
let fui = XOR(di, (h(Concat(IDui,PWui)))) in
let eui = h(Concat(IDui,(PWui,Bui)))in
let gui = XOR(Li, (h(Concat(PWui,IDui))))in
(*************Login-authentication***********)
event start_UI(IDui);
let Bistar = Mult(BK,(h(fngui))) in
if Bistar = Mult(BK,(h(fngui))then
let eistar = (h(Concat(IDui,(PWui,Bui)))) in
if eistar = (h(Concat(IDui,(PWui,Bui)))) then
let distar = XOR(fui, h(Concat(IDui,PWui))) in
let Listar= XOR(gi, h(XOR (PWui,IDui))) in
new T1: bitstring;
new SCNj: bitstring;
```

```
let M1 = XOR(IDui, h(Concat(Li,T1))) in
let M2 = XOR(ri, h(Concat( distar,T1))) in
let M3 = h(Concat(distar,(ri,T1))) in
let SCTx = XOR(SCNj, h(T1)) in
let EIDj = XOR(IDsn,h(Concat(IDui,(ri,T1)))) in
out(ChPub,(M1,M2,M3,T1,SCTx,EIDsn));
in (ChPub,(M4:bitstring,M5:bitstring));
let M4star = h(Concat(IDui,(distar,T1))) in
if M4star = h(Concat(IDui,(distar,T1))) then
let M6 = h(Concat(IDui,(ri,T1))) in
let SCNj = XOR(M5, Li) in
out(ChPub,(M6));
in (ChPub,(M11:bitstring,M12:bitstring));
let Rsnstar = XOR(M11, ri) in
let SKi = h(Concat(IDui,(IDsn,ri,Rsnstar))) in
new rs: bitstring;
let M12star = h(Concat(SK,(IDui,di,rs))) in
if M12star = h(Concat(SK,(IDui,di,rs))) then
event end_UI(IDui)
else
0.
let pGN=
event start_GN(IDGN);
in (ChPub,(M1:bitstring,M2:bitstring,M3:bitstring,SCTx:bitstring,EIDsn:bitstring));
new T1:bitstring;
new XGN:bitstring;
let SCNj = XOR(SCTx ,h(T1)) in
let Li' =h(Concat(SCN,XGN)) in
let IDui' = XOR(M1, h(Concat(Li',T1))) in
let di' = h(Concat(IDui',Xgn)) in
let ri' = XOR( M2, h(Concat(di', T1))) in
let M3' = h(Concat(di',(ri',T1))) in
if M3' = h(Concat(di',(ri',T1))) then
let M4 = h(Concat (IDui,(di',T1))) in
new EXGN:bitstring;
new ri:bitstring;
```

```
new T2:bitstring;
let SCNjnew = Mult(EXGN, Concat(SCN,ri)) in
let M5 = XOR(SCNjnew, Li') in
out(ChPub,(M4,M5));
in (ChPub,(M6:bitstring));
let M6' = h(Concat(di' ,(IDui',ri',T1))) in
let IDj' = XOR(EIDj, h(Concat(IDui,(ri,T1)))) in
let Xsn' =h(Concat(IDsn',Xgn)) in
let M7 = h(Concat(IDui, (IDsn', IDGN, Xsn', ri' ,T2))) in
let M8 = XOR(IDui',h(Concat(IDGN, (Xsn,T2))))in
let M9 = XOR(ri, h(Concat(IDui, Xsn'))) in
out(ChPub,(IDGN,M7,M8,M9,T2));
in (ChPub,(M10:bitstring,M11:bitstring,T3:bitstring));
let rs' = XOR(M11, ri) in
let SKGN = h(Concat(IDui',(IDui,ri',rs')))in
new rs:bitstring;
let M10'= h(Concat(SKGN,(Xsn ,rs ,T3))) in
if M10'= h(Concat(SKGN,(Xsn ,rs ,T3))) then
let M12 = h(Concat(SKGN,(IDui',rs))) in
out(ChPub,(M11,M12));
event end_GN(IDGN)
else
0.
let pXsn=
(***********Registration phase*************)
in (ChSec,(xIDui:bitstring));
let di = h(Concat(IDui,Xgn)) in
let Li = h(Concat(SCN,Xgn)) in
new r0:bitstring;
new EXgn:bitstring;
let SCNj = Mult(EXgn, Concat(SCN,r0)) in
(**********Login-authentication*************)
event start_Xsn(IDsn);
new T2:bitstring;
new Rs:bitstring;
in (ChPub,(xIDGN:bitstring,M7:bitstring,M8:bitstring,M9:bitstring,T3:bitstring));
```

```
let IDuistr = XOR(M8, h(Concat(IDGN,(Xsn,T2)))) in
let ristr = XOR(M9, h(Concat(IDuistr,Xsn))) in
let M7str = h(Concat(IDuistr, (IDsn,IDGN,Xsn,T2))) in
if M7str = h(Concat(IDuistr, (IDsn,IDGN,Xsn,T2))) then
let SKsn = h(Concat(IDuistr ,(IDsn,Ristr,Rs))) in
let M10 = h(Concat(SKsn,(Xsn ,rs ,T3))) in
let M11 = XOR(ristr , rs) in
out(ChPub,(M10,M11,T3));
event end_Xsn(IDsn)
else
0.
process ((!pXsn) | (!pGN) | (!pUI) )
```

Output of the Proposed Protocol

```
 Query inj-event(end_SN(IDsn[])) ==> inj-event(start_Sn(IDsn[]))
Completing...
Starting query inj-event(end_S(IDsn[])) ==> inj-event(start_SN(IDsn[]))
RESULT inj-event(end_SN(IDsn[])) ==> inj-event(start_SN(IDsn[])) is true.
-- Query inj-event(end_GN(IDGN[])) ==> inj-event(start_GN(IDGN[]))
Completing...
Starting query inj-event(end_GN(IDGN[])) ==> inj-event(start_GN(IDGN[]))
RESULT inj-event(end_GN(IDGN[])) ==> inj-event(start_GN(IDGN[])) is true.
-- Query inj-event(end_UI(IDui[])) ==> inj-event(start_UI(IDui[]))
Completing...
Starting query inj-event(end_UI(IDui[])) ==> inj-event(start_UI(IDui[]))
RESULT inj-event(end_UI(IDui[])) ==> inj-event(start_UI(IDui[])) is true.
-- Query not attacker(SK[])
Completing...
Starting query not attacker(SK[])
RESULT not attacker(SK[]) is true.
```

4.2   Informal Security Analysis

In this part of security scrutiny we check the robustness, accuracy and security of the proposed protocol against all possible attacked, specially mentioned in chapter 3 of the thesis. Our proposed scheme is verified that this protocol is tackling all possible well-known attacks. Deem an adversary can interrupt a system, which can change the communication information, copy a part of communications message, resend the messages, or deliver false objects etc. This hypothesis is collective for everybody and also more sensible in modern era. Our proposed scheme accomplished the following possible security hazard which is narrated as under:-

4.2.1   User Anonymity

As identity protection and privacy concern is growing among the individuals. As in private and government organization the privacy and anonymity is important research topic in the recent era. In distant authentication protocol the user anonymity is define as "who is the Initiator, Transmitter anonymity more specifically means that the opponent might not have the information of the actual identification of the originator but may recognize whether two dialogue initiate from the similar (unidentified) entity. So this protocol protect the individual personal information to accomplished user anonymity[32]. Here in Amin et al.'s protocol, the SCT_x is transmitted over the public channel, thus $SCT_x = SC_N \oplus h(T_1)$ in this message the unique smartcard number SCN is transmitted in plain. Hence from this message the initiator/sender information may breach so this problem may lead to violation of user anonymity such as:

$SCT_x = SC_N \oplus h(T_1)$

But here in the proposed protocol we encrypted the unique smartcard number SCN with private key of GN and then send on the public channel:- $SCN_j = X_{GN}(SCN||r_i)$ then send SCN_j in encrypted form. The adversary $\mathcal{A}$ may possibly attempt for the extraction of the identity ID_{ui} of the user U_i wither for the public channel or from the smartcard. However the same is infeasible for the adversary $\mathcal{A}$ because of the identity protection by different means in the proposed protocol. Thus the above discussions reveal that our scheme can resist the user anonymity and off-line ID guessing attack.

4.2.2 User Untraceability

User traceability is vulnerable issue for secure authentication protocol because traceability may lead different attacks. $\mathcal{A}$ interrupt two dissimilar communications from the dissimilar sessions and test that they are equal. If same $\mathcal{A}$ trust that both messages send by the similar user. $\mathcal{A}$ cannot seize one or extra public messages, because the random number and timestamps is different in every session as well the login messages of every session are besides different. Hence, our protocol opposes user un-traceability attacks.

4.2.3 Stolen smart-card attack

In the stolen smartcard attack $\mathcal{A}$ getting the confidential information from the smartcard by using the mechanism of extracting information given[33][34]. Assume that normally U_i using low entropy using only ID and password, imagine that guess or find out in a polynomial time. But $\mathcal{A}$ try not just to extract secret information, however it need to get ID and password which is not possible in this protocol because of the following properties:-

> Suppose $\mathcal{A}$ extract the smartcard information $(B_{ui}, e_{ui}, f_{ui}, g_{ui}, SC_N, BK())$ from the smartcard but these parameters are encrypted with XOR operation and simple hash function, whereas $B_{ui} = BK(H(fng_{ui}))$ $e_{ui} = h(ID_{ui}||PW_{ui}||B_{ui}), f_{ui} = d_i \oplus h(ID_{ui}||PW_{ui})$ and $g_{ui} = L_i \oplus h(PW_{ui} \oplus ID_{ui})$, it show that d_i unidentified to $\mathcal{A}$ in the same way $\mathcal{A}$ cannot compute g_{ui} without the value of L_i because these value are secured by hash function.Therefore $\mathcal{A}$ is not able to extract successful the required value due to unpredictability of hash function

In view of the above it is so clear that the attacker not able to get the confidential information from the stolen smartcard. So, our scheme is safe against the stolen smartcard attack.

4.2.4 Replay Attack

In cryptography, opposing the replay attack is pretty hard. In our novel scheme the adversary may possibly try to forge older messages with no changes of the communicating participant e.g. (user, gate-way node and the sensor-node). In broad, the timestamp techniques are used for the resistance of replay attacks, but maintain time synchronization crosswise huge networks is pretty complicated. It must be remember that WSN network are applied on a particular area, so reducing the same time synchronization issue. Hence, the timestamp method can only be applied for GN and SN. We use the timestamp mechanism in GN and

SN, where GN and SN verify the validity of the time-stamps by computing at all security restriction. If $\mathcal{A}$ make fakes the earlier messages of the communicating participant, the protocol close-up the link due to invalid timestamp.

Still, preserving time synchronization within big net works is tough. Particularly, the access of users services from some-where, or from the communication infrastructure. So, the timestamp techniques are not suitable for tackling replay attacks especially involving user. While the protocol cannot use the time-stamp mechanism among the users and the getaway nodes, $\mathcal{A}$ may possibly try to instigate the replay attack, although will be unsuccessful because:

1. Suppose that $\mathcal{A}$ replays the older message $MSG_1 = (M_1, M_2, M_3, T_1, SCT_x, EID_{SN})$ to GN without any alterations.

2. It is well-known that the repeated messages should be authenticated by GN. In our protocol, GN send out $MSG_2 = (M_4, M_5)$ to U_i GN and SN suppose that $\mathcal{A}$ interrupt $MSG_2 = (M_4, M_5)$ this message from the unreliable channel.

3. $\mathcal{A}$ computes a valid M_6, which is contingent on the identity ID_{ui}, secret parameter d_i as well the random no r_i. We already shown that $\mathcal{A}$ has not capable to get ID_{ui}, r_i, d_i, as $\mathcal{A}$ is not able to get any information, calculations of the valid M_6 is not possible. $\mathcal{A}$ convey M_6 to GN after deduction the necessary parameters, GN finish the link because M_6 is invalid.

4.2.5   Off-line password guessing attack

Similar to the identity guessing in off-line, $\mathcal{A}$ be able to get the password of a user U_i in polynomial time. In this scheme, we have verified that $\mathcal{A}$ is not capable to find out the password PW_{ui} of U_i by means of smart-card information. Especially, the public channel messages of the novel scheme are free from PW_{ui}. Thus, finding or extracting PW_{ui} from the messages of the public channel is unrealistic in our protocol.

4.2.6   User-impersonation attack

In this kind of attack $\mathcal{A}$ interrupt the login credential of the protocol, in that case $\mathcal{A}$ attempt to formulate another fake login message. But here in the proposed protocol $\mathcal{A}$ is unable to do so. Suppose $\mathcal{A}$ interrupt the login message $MSG_1 = \{M_1, M_2, M_3, T_1, SCT_x, EID_{SN}\}$, where $SCT_x = SC_N \oplus h(T_1)$, $M_1 = ID_{ui}^* \oplus h(L_i^* \| T_1)$, $M_2 = r_i \oplus h(d_i^* \| T_i$, $M_3 = h(d_i^* \| r_i \| T_1)$ and $EID_{SN} = ID_{SN} \oplus h(ID_{ui} \| r_i \| T_1)$. So it show that $\mathcal{A}$ can take a new random number with time timestamp but $\mathcal{A}$ needs the identity of user ID_{ui}, sensor node ID_{SN} as well the L_i to compute the afore mentioned values respectively. In this regard $\mathcal{A}$ needs d_i to computes M_2, M_3 so $\mathcal{A}$ is not able to extract the same without the (ID_{ui}, ID_{SN}, d_i). Therefore, our scheme provides security against user-impersonation attack.

4.2.7   Gateway node impersonation attack

This attack is same like the user impersonation attack, in which $\mathcal{A}$ might attempt to masquerade as GN after interrupting validation messages during the execution of the protocol. So to do so the same, $\mathcal{A}$ require to computes $(M_4, ID_{GN}, M_7, M_8, M_9, T_2)$, where $M_7 = h(ID'_{ui}||ID'_{SN}||ID_{GN}||S'_{SN}||r'_i||T_2)$, $M_8 = ID' \oplus h(ID_{GN}||S'_{SN}||T_2)$ and $M_9 = r_i \oplus h(ID'_{ui}||S'_{SN})$. Thus $\mathcal{A}$ require $(ID_{ui}, ID_{SN}, S_{SN})$ for the computation of M_7, M_8 and M_9 respectively. Since these identities $(ID_{ui}, ID_{SN}, S_{SN})$ are unidentified so it show that it is infeasible to compute other successful forge authentication message. Hence, this protocol provides full security against gateway node impersonation.

4.2.8   Sensor node impersonation attack

Just like gateway node impersonation attack the sensor node SN may also impersonated by $\mathcal{A}$ after erupting the authentication message. $\mathcal{A}$ needs to create $MSG_5 = (M_{10}, M_{11}, T_3)$ to interrupt SN, where $SK_{SN} = h(ID^{**}_{ui}||ID_{SN}||r^{**}_i||r_s)$, $M_{10} = h(SK_{SN}||X_{SN}||r_s||T_3)$ and $M_{11} = (r^{**}_i \oplus r_s)$. Therefore, $\mathcal{A}$ needs $(ID_{ui}, ID_{SN}, X_{SN}, r_i)$ to calculate $MSG_5 = (M_{10}, M_{11}, T3)$. While $\mathcal{A}$ has still no knowledge about the $(ID_{ui}, ID_{SN}, S_{SN}, r_i)$, so it is impossible to lunch the sensor node impersonation attack.

4.2.9   Privileged-insider attack

If the malicious user or an insider of the organization obtains the user password by various means, he or she lunched a privileged-insider attack to break other schemes by using the same password and identity to register. The malicious users generally utilize the same identity and password for sets of servers. As per the information of the literature, the majority security schemes are susceptible to this insider attack. So, this attack is a vital attack in password-based authentication schemes. During the registration of the user in our scheme, U_i sends only ID_{ui} in registration phase public messages are free of U_i password. Hence, an insider malicious user has no way to get U_i password.

4.2.10   Session key computation attack

In this authentication protocol the session key is obviously use for encryption of secret information the transmissions of message between the entities on unreliable channel. The key characteristic of the session key is novelty and freshness, so it means that the session key should be different for every session. In our proposed scheme, U_i, GN and SN negotiate the sessions key $SK_{ui} = SK_{GN} = SK_{SN} = h(ID_{ui}||ID_{SN}||r_i||r_s)$ that trust on the secret message $(ID_{ui}, ID_{SN}, r_i, r_j)$ that are unidentified to $\mathcal{A}$. Thus $\mathcal{A}$ not capable to extract the requisite session key without the knowledge of $(ID_{ui}, ID_{SN}, r_i, r_j)$. Moreover, the session key in this scheme having the freshness quality because of using these random numbers (r_i, r_j).

4.2.11   Verification of the session key

Session key negotiation is verified at the time of protocol execution. In authentication phase of the protocol GN verify the session key SK_{SN} generated by the sensor nod SN with the confirmation whether $M'_{10} = M_{10}$ holds. Subsequently U_i authenticated that whether $M^*_{12} = M_{12}$ holds for verification of the session key SK_{GN} which is created by GN. Hence the proposed protocol also provides the property of session key verification.

4.2.12   Mutual Authentication

For secure communication when public message passes over unreliable channel, so mutual authentication between the participant entities must be provided. In this scheme during the protocol execution each member authenticates other. Because authentication is property of security in which all participants of a protocol uniformly authenticates each other at matching time. Our protocol achieves every circumstances of mutual authentication moreover, our protocol furnished proper mutual authentication among the entire three participant entities U_i, GN and SN.

4.2.13   Man-in-Middle attack

It is that type of security attack in which a malicious user or attacker illegally entered in communication between the two parties and interrupt the communication. The adversary completely captured the secret information also can send or receive messages any time by impersonating both communicating parties by imagining itself a legal user of the organization.

In our proposed protocol the attacker or the adversaries not able to do the Man-In-Middle attack because in our proposed protocol exist mutual authentication on each side of endpoint. We use timestamps with every message also the time difference is checked at end point if valid then proceed the communication or otherwise. We also use random number so adversary not-able to guess any public key or secret random number from which attacker can find out the session key moreover, our session key establishment is completely fair. Hence, our proposed scheme can protect the Man-In-Middle attacks.

4.2.14   Protection of unauthorized login

The user un-intentionally tries to enter incorrect information at the smart-card device during the login phase. Due to this wrong information the protocol perform additional computation and the congestion of network rising. Therefore, in this initial stage wrong information should be protected at login phase to avoid additional execution of protocol. Hence the terminal should not create a login message without authentication of a user legality. So in our scheme the likelihood of providing erroneous information is not possible in biometric information/data instead of password information. Though if user given the wrong finger-print fng_i then the condition in the login phase $(B_{ui}^* \neq B_{ui})$ not hold then the session abort, whereas $B_{ui}^* = BK(H(fng_i))$. Suppose that U_i enter the right finger-print, however in case of password when enter the incorrect password PW_{ui}, the smart-card can reject the user login message, because $(e_{ui}^* \neq e_{ui})$ where $e_{ui}^* = h(ID_{ui}||PW_{ui}||B_{ui})$.

4.2.15   Provision of Post-deployment phase

This phase is essential when the sensor node on the target region may occur damage due to some way so it needs to replace the same. Moreover the target area some time needs to expend the network. So SA deploy the requisite sensor nodes and expanded the target field, for the provision of this facility the addendum scheme offer this post deployment phase to do so.

4.3   Chapter Summary

In this chapter we examine the security assessment of proposed scheme that how to do its function in look of aggressive intruder. In generally we discuss two types of security analysis;

formal and informal that may possibly or may not formulate use of automatic tools. In formal analysis we used the ProVerif tool for which using the pi-calculus for checking the protocol security and robustness. In informal analysis offers less assertion than the formal. Despite that it is also may give better scope, because there are security weaknesses that still we are not able to know how to model mathematically. So a formal analysis offers a large degree of guarantee than an informal analysis, but it only trusts on hypothesis regarding the cryptographic algorithms exercise that could not be probable to verify.

Chapter 5

Performance and Security comparison

In this chapter we assist and determine various characteristics, such as computational cost, communication cost and storage cost of the proposed scheme and compare with the previous related already existing protocols[1,2,5,30]. We have shown the result of the proposed and previous protocol in the tables 5.1, 5.2, 5.3, 5.4 for the measurement of clear efficiency of our protocol. The novel protocol resists all known threats, having the requisite functionality but with some high complexity. We examine the efficiency of proposed protocol in the following terms:-

- Security features comparison
- Computational Cost
- Communication Cost
- Storage Cost

5.1   Security features comparison

The comparison of propose scheme are shown in the following table in which the proposed scheme resist all known threats. We compared all 13 requisite security features of our proposed protocol with the previous related schemes [1,2,5,30] whereas, R is resistance against possible threats which started from R1 and so on. The comparison table shows that only our scheme provides all 13 requirements. The detailed comparison is shown in table.

Requirements	[5]	[30]	[2]	[1]	Proposed Scheme
R1	×	×	✓	✓	✓
R2	×	×	✓	✓	✓
R3	×	✓	✓	✓	✓
R4	✓	✓	✓	✓	✓
R5	×	✓	✓	✓	✓
R6	×	✓	✓	✓	✓
R7	✓	×	✓	✓	✓
R8	✓	✓	✓	✓	✓
R9	×	✓	✓	×	✓
R10	×	×	×	✓	✓
R11	×	×	×	✓	✓
R12	×	×	×	✓	✓
R13	×	×	×	✓	✓

Table 5.1: Security requirements table

- R1:User anonymity.
- R2:User untraceability.
- R3:Stolen Smartcard attack .
- R4:Replay Attack.
- R5:Offline-Password guessing attack.
- R6:Impersonation Attack.
- R7:Privileged Insider Attack.
- R8:Verification of the Session Key.
- R9:Man-in-the middle Attack.
- R10:Provision of Post deployment phase.
- R11:Identity Change Phase.
- R12:Appropriate Mutual Authentication.
- R13:Smartcard Revocation.

| ✓: Yes Resist, ×: Does not Resist |

5.2   Computation Cost Analysis

Energy consumption is a big issue in WSN therefore, we use mostly simple hash function and
XOR operations. The computation cost of a few lightweight function such as XOR operations
and concatenations are so small due to its tiny computation cost so we ignore these lightweight
functions. Our main concentration is to scrutinize cryptographic functions that U_i, SN and
GN require to execute. One-way hash function is simple to implement also take small time
as compare to other operations. The symmetric encryption and decryption takes three time
more cost than hash operation[2], Amin et al.[1]has not been using encryption/decryption
but in our proposed scheme we use one time symmetric encryption/decryption to secure the
security loophole of Amin et al. scheme therefore the running time of our proposed scheme
is slightly greater than Amin et al. [1] as shown in the table 5.2. We deem all three contri-
butor U_i, SN and GN. Detailed explanation is illustrated in table the given notations are used:

- CC:Computation cost
- Th: CC of single hash function;
- Tse: CC of symmetric encryption;
- Tsd: CC of symmetric decryption;

5.3   Communication Cost Analysis

In this subsection we present the communication cost of our proposed protocol. The communication cost of any protocol is depending on extent of received and conveys messages. When
the network congestion are reduced and the communication message is transmitted swiftly
then the communication cost also become low down as possible. In our proposed scheme
U_i transmit 896 bits and received 384 bits, GN transmit 1152 bits and received 1280 bits
and SN transmit 384 bits and received 640 bits. So, the overall communication cost of U_i,
GN and SN are1280, 2304 and 1024 bits respectively. The communication cost is actually
the cycle of victorious communication of messages which exchange between the user and
IOT part means sensor nodes and gateway node (WSN). So our proposed scheme contained
total 6 messages/steps during successful execution. We summarize the communication cost
comparison of our proposed protocol with other related protocol in table 5.3 which almost
better than [2,5,30] but the communicational cost of proposed scheme almost similar with

Computation Cost	[5]	[30]	[2]	[1]	Proposed Scheme
CC_{U_i}	7Th	11Th	15Th	12Th	12Th
CC_{SN}	5Th	8Th	10Th	5Th	5Th
CC_{GN}	7Th	14Th	0Th	15Th	15Th
CC_{Total}	19Th	32Th	25Th	32Th	32Th+1tse+1tsd
RT	0.0076 ms	0.0128 ms	0.01 ms	0.0128 ms	0.1431 ms

Table 5.2: Comparison of computation cost and running time

CC_{U_i}: Computation Cost of U_i
CC_{SN} : Computation Cost of SN
CC_{GN} : Computation Cost of GN
CC_{total}: Total computation Cost
RT: Running Time

the Amin et al.[1] scheme because the transmission and receiving of bits are same among the entities as well the exchanging of messages also same.

5.4   Storage Cost Analysis

The requisite property of our proposed scheme to reduce the storage cost of smart car and the sensor-node. So, the storage cost of the sensor-node and user smart card are very small than

Schemes	Ui	GN	SN	Total	Messages
Turkanovic et al.[5]	1404	1792	3200	6396	4
Farash et al.[30]	1152	1664	2816	5632	4
Ruhal and Biswas[2]	1408	2432	1280	5120	4
R.Amin et al.[1]	1280	2304	1024	4608	6
Proposed Scheme	1280	2304	1024	4608	6

Table 5.3: Communication Cost of Proposed and other Protocols

Schemes	Storage Cost
Turkanovic et al.[5]	768
Farash et al.[30]	512
Ruhal and Biswas [2]	640
R.Amin et al.[1]	640
Proposed Scheme	640

Table 5.4: Storage Cost Analysis

the gateway node of the proposed protocol. Energy conservation is the big issue in WSN so the sensor node communication cost should be minimum. We analyze the storage cost especially at the sensor node. The storage cost is higher in [5] but in the other comparative scheme [1,2] the storage cost is relatively same. We preferred MD5 therefore, we imagine that the size of password, identity, hash function and random number are 128 bits. Hence the smart card storage our protocol is relatively equal to [1,2] as shown in the Table 5.4.

5.5   Chapter Summary

In this chapter we represented the efficiency of the proposed scheme and compare the same with the previous related scheme. The result of proposed scheme is analyze in the term of computation cost, communication cost and storage cost. All the performance are shown in the appropriate tables.

Chapter 6

Conclusion and Future Work

In this thesis, we inspected Amin et al.'s protocol in which we examined that this protocol having some security loopholes in terms of anonymity and traceability attacks. In order to protect the security flaws of the said protocol, this thesis has primarily accomplished a novel robust light weight three-factor user authentication and session key agreement protocol for WSNs in which the user can securely access the real time information from the IOT environment. Moreover, to verify its security perfection, we simulated the novel protocol in BAN-Logic and most popular accepted security simulation tool ProVerif. The results of this enhanced protocol show that the same protocol provides security against all active as well passive attacks. Likewise, informal security analysis and comparison also revealed that this improved scheme is safe against all threat. High communication and computation cost are major challenges in authentication of WSN based IoT. In future our goal is to work on the efficiency of WSN in terms of low communication and computation cost in WSN environment.

Bibliography

[1] Amin R, Islam SH, Biswas G, Khan MK, Leng L, Kumar N. Design of an anonymity-preserving three-factor authenticated key exchange protocol for wireless sensor networks. *Computer Networks* 2016; **101**:42–62.

[2] Amin R, Biswas G. A secure light weight scheme for user authentication and key agreement in multi-gateway based wireless sensor networks. *Ad Hoc Networks* 2016; **36**:58–80.

[3] Khan I, Belqasmi F, Glitho R, Crespi N, Morrow M, Polakos P. Wireless sensor network virtualization: Early architecture and research perspectives. *IEEE Network* 2015; **29**(3):104–112.

[4] Vaidya B, Chen M, Rodrigues JJ. Improved robust user authentication scheme for wireless sensor networks. *Wireless Communication and Sensor Networks (WCSN), 2009 Fifth IEEE Conference on*, IEEE, 2009; 1–6.

[5] Turkanović M, Brumen B, Hölbl M. A novel user authentication and key agreement scheme for heterogeneous ad hoc wireless sensor networks, based on the internet of things notion. *Ad Hoc Networks* 2014; **20**:96–112.

[6] Tseng HR, Jan RH, Yang W. An improved dynamic user authentication scheme for wireless sensor networks. *IEEE GLOBECOM 2007-IEEE Global Telecommunications Conference*, IEEE, 2007; 986–990.

[7] Huang X, Xiang Y, Chonka A, Zhou J, Deng RH. A generic framework for three-factor authentication: Preserving security and privacy in distributed systems. *IEEE Transactions on Parallel and Distributed Systems* 2011; **22**(8):1390–1397.

[8] Childs JR. *General solution of the ADFGVX Cipher System*. Aegean Park Press, 2002.

[9] Fan R, Ping LD, Fu JQ, Pan XZ. A secure and efficient user authentication protocol for

two-tiered wireless sensor networks. *Circuits, Communications and System (PACCS), 2010 Second Pacific-Asia Conference on*, vol. 1, IEEE, 2010; 425–428.

[10] Agrawal M, Mishra P. A comparative survey on symmetric key encryption techniques. *International Journal on Computer Science and Engineering* 2012; **4**(5):877.

[11] Stallings W. *Cryptography and network security: principles and practices*. Pearson Education India, 2006.

[12] Stallings W. *Cryptography and network security: principles and practices*. Pearson Education India, 2006.

[13] Simon DR. Finding collisions on a one-way street: Can secure hash functions be based on general assumptions? *International Conference on the Theory and Applications of Cryptographic Techniques*, Springer, 1998; 334–345.

[14] Lumini A, Nanni L. An improved biohashing for human authentication. *Pattern recognition* 2007; **40**(3):1057–1065.

[15] Radha N, Karthikeyan S. An evaluation of fingerprint security using noninvertible biohash. *International Journal of Network Security & Its Applications* 2011; **3**(4).

[16] Chaudhry SA, Naqvi H, Farash MS, Shon T, Sher M. An improved and robust biometrics-based three factor authentication scheme for multiserver environments. *The Journal of Supercomputing* 2015; :1–17.

[17] Watro R, Kong D, Cuti Sf, Gardiner C, Lynn C, Kruus P. Tinypk: securing sensor networks with public key technology. *Proceedings of the 2nd ACM workshop on Security of ad hoc and sensor networks*, ACM, 2004; 59–64.

[18] Wong KH, Zheng Y, Cao J, Wang S. A dynamic user authentication scheme for wireless sensor networks. *IEEE International Conference on Sensor Networks, Ubiquitous, and Trustworthy Computing (SUTC'06)*, vol. 1, IEEE, 2006; 8–pp.

[19] He D, Gao Y, Chan S, Chen C, Bu J. An enhanced two-factor user authentication scheme in wireless sensor networks. *Ad Hoc & Sensor Wireless Networks* 2010; **10**(4):361–371.

[20] Das ML. Two-factor user authentication in wireless sensor networks. *IEEE Transactions on Wireless Communications* 2009; **8**(3):1086–1090.

[21] Vaidya B, Rodrigues JJ, Park JH. User authentication schemes with pseudonymity for ubiquitous sensor network in ngn. *International Journal of Communication Systems* 2010; **23**(9-10):1201–1222.

[22] Khan MK, Alghathbar K. Cryptanalysis and security improvements of Štwo-factor user authentication in wireless sensor networksŠ. *Sensors* 2010; **10**(3):2450–2459.

[23] Yuan J, Jiang C, Jiang Z. A biometric-based user authentication for wireless sensor networks. *Wuhan University Journal of Natural Sciences* 2010; **15**(3):272–276.

[24] Xu J, Zhu WT, Feng DG. An improved smart card based password authentication scheme with provable security. *Computer Standards & Interfaces* 2009; **31**(4):723–728.

[25] Yeh HL, Chen TH, Liu PC, Kim TH, Wei HW. A secured authentication protocol for wireless sensor networks using elliptic curves cryptography. *Sensors* 2011; **11**(5):4767–4779.

[26] Bonchi F, Lakshmanan LV, Wang HW. Trajectory anonymity in publishing personal mobility data. *ACM Sigkdd Explorations Newsletter* 2011; **13**(1):30–42.

[27] Das AK, Sharma P, Chatterjee S, Sing JK. A dynamic password-based user authentication scheme for hierarchical wireless sensor networks. *Journal of Network and Computer Applications* 2012; **35**(5):1646–1656.

[28] Turkanovic M, Holbl M. An improved dynamic password-based user authentication scheme for hierarchical wireless sensor networks. *Elektronika ir Elektrotechnika* 2013; **19**(6):109–116.

[29] Li CT, Weng CY, Lee CC. An advanced temporal credential-based security scheme with mutual authentication and key agreement for wireless sensor networks. *Sensors* 2013; **13**(8):9589–9603.

[30] Farash MS, Turkanović M, Kumari S, Hölbl M. An efficient user authentication and key agreement scheme for heterogeneous wireless sensor network tailored for the internet of things environment. *Ad Hoc Networks* 2016; **36**:152–176.

[31] Kyntaja T. A logic of authentication by burrows, abadi and needham. *Science Helsinki University of Technology, Tehran. http://www. tml. tkk. fi/Opinnot/Tik-110.501/1995/ban. html* 1995; .

[32] Wang D, Ma Cg, Shi L, Wang Yh. On the security of an improved password authentication scheme based on ecc. *International Conference on Information Computing and Applications*, Springer, 2012; 181–188.

[33] Kocher P, Jaffe J, Jun B. Differential power analysis. *Annual International Cryptology Conference*, Springer, 1999; 388–397.

[34] Messerges TS, Dabbish EA, Sloan RH. Examining smart-card security under the threat of power analysis attacks. *IEEE transactions on computers* 2002; **51**(5):541–552.